Looking for Moral Guidance

Dilemma and the Bible

James A. Fischer, C.M.

PAULIST PRESS
New York/Mahwah

Copyright © 1992 by James A. Fischer

Library of Congress Cataloging-in-Publication Data

Fischer, James A.
    Looking for moral guidance : dilemma and the Bible / James A. Fischer.
        p.   cm.
    Includes bibliographical references.
    ISBN 0-8091-3170-6
    1. Christian ethics—Catholic authors.   2. Ethics in the Bible.
I. Title.
BJ1249.F543   1992
341'.042—dc20   92-35933
                                                                      CIP

Published by Paulist Press
997 Macarthur Boulevard
Mahwah, New Jersey 07430

Printed and bound in the
United States of America

2-19-93

Contents

Introduction

This is a simple proposal for bringing scripture to bear on our ethical decision making. It requires relatively little theory but much sensitivity to biblical literature and to the art of living with open eyes.

We start with images. Most of our decisions are made on the basis of images. That is one of our few theories but we all know something about it from our own experience. Scripture deals mostly with images; stories are its stock in trade. Both the biblical stories and our own experiences involve a conflict. The crux is to identify what the true conflict really is. We generally need to escalate it so that it is something really worthwhile. Our biblical stories usually do so; our real-life problems should end up by asking: "Where is God in this mess?" So we try to find a biblical story which throws light on our present story. This requires some artistry on both levels—the sensitivity spoken of above.

The biblical story almost always leads to a demand for faith. The community of faith helps us along the road. The church is the first teacher. By the teacher we do not mean precisely the people in Rome; they are not the judges, the legislators, the arresting officers or the jailers. They are teachers within a teaching church. There are other kinds of teachers from philosophers to umpires who are associated with other traditions of law—natural law, ecclesiastical law, civil law, customs, family codes, rules for playing baseball, football, etc. They help us especially in the normal categories of decisions. Sometimes we are called upon to make big decisions which transcend the ordinary. Then faith becomes clearly a leap in the dark, without logical proof that we are right. Only at the moment when our Christian faith enters into the decision making do we become Christian in action.

Our final step is to discover a person. We are still searching Eden for the tree of knowledge, still looking for how we can become like God. We talk about the decalogue as the supreme law. We should note that the term means "ten words." Words reveal. It is not the code which is revealed at the end but the person behind the code. There we discover God and there we discover who we truly are. Where our decisions coincide with those of the community, we have security. Sometimes we must venture out on our own as free people; then we must be sure that we are being totally honest. At that terrifying moment we know how much we need God.

This is a simple enough way of doing things. It does involve a constant comparison between our story and the stories in the Bible. The connection is largely in the story-telling, not in the content of specific decisions. The Bible is full of a consciousness of story-telling even when it is giving instructions or reflections or praising God. The preacher is revealed not so much by what is said as by the selection and manner in which it is said. We find the preacher dull, cold, stand-offish or conversely interesting, right on the mark, warmly sharing, etc. We are constantly making speeches to ourselves, telling ourselves our own story as we remember, debate with ourselves, worry, make conclusions and act. Can we see both the biblical data and our own acting as story-telling?

1

The Nurse's Story

Lucille was finished for the day and made one last check as she went down the corridor, just noting if all the familiar things were in place. She was not scrupulous but she liked to be sure that everything was in order. Even if she was not the housekeeper, a job was a job and she was very conscious of her responsibilities—as well as those of others.

At her apartment there was a note from Judy. Of all the people she worked with at the hospital, unpredictable, eccentric Judy was her closest friend—probably because she was so different. As soon as she got settled, she called Judy.

"Hi, Lou," Judy said in her off-hand way. Then the usual amenities of sparring-around. "How about changing duty with me?" she finally got around to the business at hand.

"Sure. When?" Lucille asked.

"Tomorrow like—I know it's sudden, but I got this one chance to go out with this real great guy on his boat. He's just in town for one day."

"OK," Lucille said instinctively. "What you got on?"

"Usual stuff with Dr. Henderson," Judy filled her in. "Nothing big."

"Doesn't Henderson do abortions?" Lucille asked.

"Yeah, I guess so," Judy answered nonchalantly. "He might have one."

"You know I don't like abortions, Judy," Lucille said. They had had several sensational fights about it before. Lucille had not made it known at the hospital that she wanted to be exempted from abortions—she didn't want to be considered one of "them." For some reason she just didn't like assisting at abortions and she really didn't know why. It was certainly not a matter of principle with her—if she could identify any "principles" it would probably have been on the side of a woman's rights. But she just didn't like it and tried to avoid it as much as possible.

"Oh, come on, Lou," Judy cajoled. "It's only one little procedure and it's not the whole day's work."

"No," and Lucille found herself stamping her foot. She wondered now whether she should not have let it be known that she did not want to assist at abortions. The hospital had provided a noble way out for her.

"Come on, girl," Judy was saying. "You ought to learn how to handle your prejudices. Do you good."

"It's not really that," Lucille answered, but she knew that she was weakening. So did Judy.

"This may be my whole future," Judy went on. "Just one day in the year for you, but this may be the big one for me. You wouldn't let a friend down, would you?"

"Oh, all right," Lucille conceded, although she wanted it known that she was really not giving in.

"I'll fix it all up, doll," Judy said, and before Lucille could make a last stand, she had hung up.

The procedure went as expected and was over rather shortly. But there was the unpleasant part. At the end Lucille was aware that she was not assisting at a birth, but at something else. It was not just another tissue that had been removed. Somebody's life was involved, if only that of two people who had thought of themselves as lovers. Even cancer patients were more concerned than that about what had been removed from them.

But it was over, and as she unlocked her car on the way home she didn't know whom she was really mad at. Judy should not have pressured her. She tried being angry at Henderson—that was usually easy, but it did not work. And she was tired. Then she would blame herself. All the way home her moods kept shifting. She finally decided that being mad was the best one. Still and all there was a feeling of guilt that kept surfacing, and she couldn't quite understand why. She had violated what she had told Judy she stood for. There was that. She was a fickle woman who could be played upon to do what others wanted her to do.

She stopped to see Judy and found her eating an avocado and watching TV. It was a frustrating and angry confrontation. Judy was apparently unconcerned about it. "Thanks for helping me out," she acknowledged. "Idiot man didn't show up. Sorry and thanks for covering for me."

But when Lucille brought up the matter of the abortion, Judy said, "What's the big deal? It's all in a day's work." And that was the end of her interest in the matter.

The next morning was even worse. Now it was not simply anger at having been taken, but the guilt. Lucille could not understand why that emotional reaction was so strong. Anger was a run-of-the-mill emotion and by mid-morning it had subsided. Guilt should not have lodged so strongly in her mind. After all, saying that she would not assist at abortions had been a matter of convenience more than anything else for her. There were no grave moral scruples or religious convictions, she told herself. She had done with them long ago. She had liberated herself from the need for religious convictions; she never went to church and she certainly did not need such empty principles to make her a good surgical nurse. She was quite content with herself, somewhat cynical and somewhat lenient toward others who had strange needs for religion. And yet she could not shake the feeling. It stayed with her all day long. Every time she saw Dr. Henderson she got angry all over again. He knew what she had done—and she thought that he enjoyed her discomfort. That took the edge off her guilt. But when he walked off the scene, the terrible feeling came back.

She had three days off and wanted to get away from it all—forget the hospital and the daily problems. Especially, forget this problem. It would go away if she did not think of it. Perhaps a bit of nostalgia would cure it. She packed her car and headed for Plainsville. That is where she had come from and perhaps she could recover the exuberance and excitement of the days when she first discovered that she wanted to be a nurse. None of the family lived there now, but it was a familiar place even if far away, and she knew where she could go and what she could see.

Plainsville was not easy to find unless one knew where to look. It was so far off the beaten track that there was only a gravel road leading to it. Fortunately, there were no hospitals and, in fact, not even a doctor's office today. In her youth, old Doctor Hastings had lived out his last years in a medical tradition so old that even he knew it was outmoded. Lucille drove down Main Street and through the park and past the school and finally up Elm where the old house was. That covered most of the passable streets in Plainsville. But it was pleasant and it did lift her spirits. Then as she drove past her childhood home it all came rushing back overwhelmingly.

Her mother had died here. Lucille was ten and her mother was pregnant. It was a dangerous pregnancy and her mother had, she thought now, foolishly gone ahead. She trusted in God. She said her prayers. She saw that the children got to church each Sunday. And she believed. Really believed. Not the make-believe faith of those who wanted to do the right thing. Just the unquestioned acceptance of a good God who protects. "God gives life; we must accept it with thanks," was her last word on that subject.

Lucille stopped the car, got out and leaned against a tree across the street from the old house. And suddenly she was back at that day. She could see the doctor's old car in the street. In that fatal room upstairs her mother was gasping her last. Never very strong, this pregnancy had come upon her with a heavy hand and complications which Doctor Hastings did not well understand. The child Lucille had been standing outside her mother's door. She could hear at times what were coherent shouts. "God damn you, God. Take my baby! I'll see you in hell. This is what I get for being good." It went on for a long time, becoming feeble with time. There was a final pause and a last shout of, "God, I hate you." Then there was a terrible quiet for a long while.

Doctor Hastings finally came out of the bedroom sweating and grim looking. He carried something in a towel and carefully avoided her. He came back shortly and disappeared into her mother's bedroom once again. It was not long after that he came out with her father and there was a finality about their appearance. Her father was weeping and seemed not even to notice her. But Doctor Hastings took her in his arms and said, "Baby, I'm sorry. Your mother didn't make it." He kissed her and set her down.

"You heard?" he asked.

She nodded yes. He looked at her and said, "Don't take it too much to heart. I've seen it before. Your mother was a good woman." And then he left.

She realized that that was the moment when she had given up on religion. Church was never again for her. Her mother had killed God as far as she was concerned, and she agreed with her mother. Now she got back in the car, drove to the park again and sat there weeping. She cursed God and cursed her own present situation for which she blamed him.

Finally, she turned the car back to her apartment and drove slowly home, although later on she could not remember the drive. She made herself a stiff Scotch and water and sat staring at the dingy apartment again. The emotional reversal was beginning to set in once more. She cursed herself for not having had the courage to tell Judy that she could fly a kite, that when she said something she meant it. But even that sounded hollow. She could not be angry at Judy or even at Dr. Henderson. Nothing had been a matter of conviction. Her decision to go ahead with the abortion had been merely an eruption of weakness. She really didn't care about Judy that much. She had been trying to live up to images and none of them was really an image of her.

And as the day wore on, a most odd peace came upon her. Whatever had happened, she had finally admitted the truth. She had not yet discovered her real self, but she knew that she had shed some of the delusions which she had called "principles." Perhaps she had also shed some of the delusions that all she wanted to be was a competent nurse. Honesty could not be all bad.

As she looked at the wall of the aging building next door, she began to feel that she loved that sight. It stood for all the good neighbors she knew, all the security and nesting that she had. She loved this neighborhood and she loved them. In that apartment across the areaway lived Mike and Elaine, a retired couple. They were always concerned about her. Elaine brought her pie and fresh vegetables at times. She knew their children and their grandchildren; she was almost part of the family.

On impulse she left and went next door and rang the Clancys' bell. They were both at home and glad to see her.

Mike took one look at her, hugged her and said, "Here, here, girl, there's something wrong. Sit down." He sat her down and both the Clancys waited for her. Predictably she began by crying, and when she could stop that, she said, "Is it always like this? Is this what life is all about?"

They coaxed the story out of her and listened with care to what she said. More than that, they listened to how she told the story.

"Well, now," Mike said at the end, "it's all out in the open and we know you better than we ever did. And we love you."

Elaine said, "Lucille, darling, I've gone through it. That's part of life. I cursed too when our little Mark was born as a cripple. You've just got to forgive yourself for being human. You'll live and love again."

"I hate God," Lucille said.

"No, you don't," Mike said. "You just hate yourself, and you'll get over that too. I suppose that God is still alive just as he was before your mother died."

An hour later when Lucille went home, she felt at peace. From somewhere deep inside her came the conviction that she had gone through a growing crisis. She was neither the angry person at the hospital nor the depressed and guilty person of her trip back home. She was alive and she was noble in spite of herself.

She savored the moment and allowed it to wash over her. Despite everything, the world was right, and she was good, and she fitted in the same as all the other pieces.

And then she remembered her mother again. She remembered not the tortured, screaming woman on her deathbed, but the happy, singing mother who had meant so much to her. She could hear her in the years when her father had gone through his crisis of alcoholism. Somehow her mother had picked up a phrase from him and liked to repeat it. "God didn't make dirt," she would say and then laugh appreciatively after she had corrected Lucille for some childish wrong. And then she would smile.

Lucille suddenly realized that she really did not want to be involved in abortions again. It was not a conclusion she had reasoned her way to, nor was it a matter of professional ethics. It simply bubbled up in her irrepressibly. She did believe in her happy, singing mother. And while she was being honest, she supposed that she even believed in a good God.

2

Convinced or Persuaded?

What shall we make of the nurse's story? It has something of the Bible embedded in it but only in a hidden way. How does that affect her actions and our judgment? How does it affect our judgment upon her actions? We can hardly escape the Bible in our culture even when we do not recognize it.[1] How did all those Christians in other ages and other cultures make their judgments?

Before we get deeply into this we need to consider the distinctive way in which this book shall view biblical ethics. About 460 B.C. in Syracuse, Greece, public speaking was first developed. After the devastation of a war a new egalitarian government decided to allow farmers whose land had been seized to plead their cases for the return of their property before the whole assembly of citizens. The farmers then noted an odd result. It was not always those who had the best cases who got most back. Public speaking seemed to depend for its effect upon the way in which one used language. Stories, dramatic images, sharp contrasts seemed to weigh most with the hearers. And so attention began to be given to rhetoric, for so it was called.

In the course of the centuries in Greece and Rome the need for such techniques of persuasion continued to be felt especially by lawyers in arguing cases, by politicians in attempting to persuade the democratic assembly, and by those called upon, often at religious gatherings, to decorate the occasion with praise of the gods.[2] This was rhetoric. Aristotle said it was the art of persuasion.

Slowly a separation developed between rhetoric and logic. Logic plotted the predictable and reasonable sequences which appealed to the human mind. It convinced. Philosophers especially used it to develop their theories. They took for granted that words represented reality. Plato and Aristotle both did. Plato in fact theorized that the ideas had always been there, independently of their being thought of by humans. The equating of words and reality was what made truth for them. Among the philosophers ethics became a science; it developed from principles to conclusions which were considered to represent the true state of human affairs. Then it was all put together in a system. We still have many such systems, most of them divergent.

Dramatists—and Greece produced the best we have seen—and poets obviously took the route of rhetoric. They were there to "persuade," sometimes for no weightier reason than entertainment. Oddly enough the Greeks, except for Aristophanes, were not very good at comedy. Comedy depended too much on unreasonableness, and that did not appeal strongly to the Greeks. But they were very good at tragedy and heroic tales. Tragedy aimed at stirring up pity for a hero who was led to an inevitable but sad ending. That described much of what the Greeks knew of life. Heroic tales appealed to one's sense of greatness in origin and prospects. The appeal of rhetoric was not immediately to truth but to a sense of the appropriateness of things as we experienced them.

Rhetoric and logic were never completely separated.[3] In fact, liberal education became a combination of the two. Lawyers studied philosophy and especially logic; they also studied the art of public speaking. They were aware that in a contest between logic and rhetoric, rhetoric usually won. Socrates in the *Dialogues of Plato* accuses rhetoricians of being liars. The ancient sneer that rhetoric cared not for truth was coined and has persisted until our day in the saying: "That's just rhetoric."[4] Yet rhetoric remained the basis of western liberal education from Greek times almost to the end of our seventeenth century.

The original Christian community came out of a Semitic culture which viewed everything as concrete and whole and down to earth. Its sacred books came from that viewpoint. Shortly thereafter it began to be explained and lived by Hellenistic peoples who diagnosed and made theories and had a hard time figuring out what the philosophy really meant in practice. In later centuries it was touched with barbarian exuberance, eastern mysticism, academic and political ordering, secularization, industrialization, scientific research, etc. But through it all some things remained so deeply encoded in the cultural system that they affected many of the decisions which were made. The telling of stories was one of the most important.

Christian theology, on the other hand, adopted the path of philosophy and logic. The Greek fathers of the church were truly Greek in their outlook and education. They tended to interpret the Bible, especially in sermons, from the standpoint of logic. Our definitions of the nature of Christ, the Trinity, the motherhood of Mary, and many other basic doctrines are all their accomplishments from a philosophical analysis. In ethics they were less perceptive but they did try to accommodate biblical sayings to prevailing ethical systems. Indeed, at times the biblical conclusions seemed hardly more than that.

The Bible, however, was not a Greek book but a Semitic one. Although they never used the term, Semites were much more inclined toward rhetoric than logic. In biblical times they never developed a philosophical system. When they used the word philosophy at all, they meant something different. Josephus, who was one of the few to do so, employed it to describe the Zealot party in the time of Christ—"the fourth philosophy." A violent political party is not our common understanding of a philosophical school. Paul also used it derisively of false teachers, and they were certainly not philosophy professors (cf. Col 2:8). They were people who proposed their own way of acting. The Semites told stories, they wrote and recited poetry, they conveyed clan wisdom in pithy proverbs, they listened to talk. The right word, the proper cadence, the fitting contrast were of high value. They were concrete in their thinking; they cared little for the pre-existing ideas which so enticed Plato and the Greeks. And yet they were extremely prolific in using the myths which attempted to explain the true nature of human life.

From medieval times Christian ethics tended more and more to become a philosophical discourse which began with a theoretical construct of the capabilities of the human being and ran down to practical conclusions as to what actions were appropriate in specific instances.[5] Catholic moral theology of the eighteenth and nineteenth centuries finally became a case book of specific decisions. In some ways moral theology committed the same mortal sin that rhetoric had done; it became so obsessed with distinctions and rules that it too became irrelevant. Behind it was a structure of "natural law" which had presumably always existed and which seemed to dictate the most minute details of right and wrong. In some ways it had even lost the dynamic which was in the original Aristotelian-Thomistic understanding of virtues and vices. And then it was threatened with new philosophies which denied or circumvented the natural law approach entirely. It was also challenged by "semeiotic" theories—that is, those which question whether words really represent realities or at least seek to understand what words do and what basic patterns in the mind they appeal to.

The early Protestant reformers, particularly Martin Luther and John Calvin, protested against making morality and legalism central to Christian living. "Luther saw in the self-concern of many Christians about their own perfection a dynamic that Paul had denounced."[6] It was faith, not works, which saved. The law was not the great divider between the good and the bad, and the personalism of early Protestantism seemed to offer hope for an ethic of freedom. Unfortunately, as the principle of self-determination worked itself out, there was often little difference between Christian morality and successful social living. Bonhoffer, H. Richard Niebuhr and Karl Barth in our century have protested and sought to reestablish an ethic of command which was uncompromising but sporadic as God addressed man. The older concept of an abiding self with virtues, character, identity and memory was downplayed. So also from the viewpoint of literature was story ignored, for story is not a series of discrete incidents, but a unifying whole.[7]

Vatican II called upon Catholic moralists to take a new look at the scriptures.[8] A debate has since ensued as to what really makes ethics Christian or whether such a thing even exists.[9] If ethics is a science, then it is open to all who will approach it with a scientific mind. Where then is faith? Does ethics dictate conclusions? Or is it the very process of reaching a decision?[10]

In biblical studies today, especially in the United States, we are seeing a revival of an interest in rhetorical or literary criticism.[11] Rhetoric had been done in not so much by its lack of respect for truth, as by its tendency to become overblown. Classifications of figures of speech and rules were endlessly multiplied and formalized. In the seventeenth century even personal letter writing was expected to conform to artificial norms of expression. Rhetoric had became stilted and lifeless. We are now seeing a revival of rhetoric or literary interpretation of the Bible.

It takes many forms but the general approach is sufficiently clear to have provoked a critical response from the more conventional historical critics.[12] Obviously in our commercial and political world of TV, PR, and government spokesmen, rhetoric has once again become a key art. Once again it encounters the criticism that it is a way of concealing, manipulating or distorting truth. But in the United States we are better acquainted with it than we are with philosophical logic. Those who espouse rhetorical criticism in biblical studies are usually aware of its pitfalls and yet also know its appeal.

What we are talking about here is the process by which people reach decisions. Fundamentalism may be used as a curious and enlightening example of what can go wrong in the ethical process even with the best of intentions.[13] It seems such an easy and straightforward way to get from the Bible to a contemporary situation. Fundamentalists of the type popularized by many TV evangelists seem to know clearly what a Christian should do. They strongly espouse certain traditional absolutes of morality—devotion to country, to family and to doctrinal purity. Almost all fundamentalists make a capital point out of the literal inerrancy of the Bible and constantly appeal to specific verses of the text which seem to answer the problem precisely. There is much here that is admirable and much that appeals to Americans in an age of religious ambiguity.

Unfortunately, fundamentalism on closer inspection is not a straight-line, logical path from biblical texts to ethical decisions. The meaning of an "inerrant text" is the principal problem. No text by itself is inerrant; it is inerrant only as interpreted by someone who claims to be inerrant. Usually the fundamentalist claims this inerrancy for an individual or for the group. No doubt is admitted; the text means what it says even if it says it only in a somewhat dubious English translation. In effect, this is a conclusion based on faith in the interpreter. The basis of that faith is often a desire to escape from otherwise crushing problems and complications. The great drive is to exclude fear, to be certain of one's own convictions, to be sure that one will be saved and that one knows how to achieve this.

This brief review has attempted to bring to mind a few of the ways in which Christians down through the ages have tried to apply the Bible to their moral lives. Let me now try to illustrate by a biblical story how I think the Bible itself often goes about this process.

THE STORY OF SAUL

The scene from the story which I shall cite concerns Saul and the witch of Endor (1 Sam 28). Saul was the first king of all Israel. By God's choice he was anointed by the prophet Samuel under somewhat compromising circumstances. The people demanded a king like the city monarchs of Canaanite cities who were their great enemies. Samuel was against it, for he saw that this would be a real threat to the monarchy of God. When he consulted Yahweh, God agreed with him but then told him to anoint a king anyway. So Saul was chosen by fateful plot and anointed by divine sanction as the first king. He defeated the Philistines, the primary enemy, and then the Ammonites. But on the way to military victory, he chose not to depend on God and assumed the role of priest and prophet himself. For this Samuel condemned him and foretold that the kingship would be taken from him.

Years later, after Samuel was dead, Saul once again faced

the Philistines who had come back with power. On the night before the final battle, fearful of defeat, he did a most unusual thing. He consulted a witch or "diviner" to discern what the coming day would bring. The text itself in the 28th chapter of 1 Samuel must be savored for all its details. It begins with Achish, one of the Philistine kings, speaking to David who oddly was then on the Philistine side.

1 Samuel 28

1   In those days the Philistines mustered their military forces to fight against Israel. So Achish said to David, "You realize, of course, that you and your men must go out on campaign with me to Jezreel."

2   David answered Achish, "Good! Now you shall learn what your servant can do." Then Achish said to David, "I shall appoint you for my permanent bodyguard."

3   Now Samuel had died and, after being mourned by all Israel, was buried in his city, Ramah. Meanwhile Saul had driven mediums and fortune-tellers out of the land.

4   The Philistine levies advanced to Shunem and encamped. Saul, too, mustered all Israel; they camped on Gilboa.

5   When Saul saw the camp of the Philistines, he was dismayed and lost heart completely.

6   He therefore consulted the Lord; but the Lord gave no answer, whether in dreams or by the Urim or through prophets.

7   Then Saul said to his servants, "Find me a woman who is a medium, to whom I can go and seek counsel through her." His servants answered him, "There is a woman in Endor who is a medium."

8   So he disguised himself, putting on other clothes, and set out with two companions. They came to the woman by night, and Saul said to her, "Tell my fortune through a ghost; conjure up for me the one I ask you to."

9   But the woman answered him, "You are surely aware of

what Saul has done, in driving the mediums and fortune-tellers out of the land. Why, then, are you laying snares for my life to have me killed?"

10   But Saul swore to her by the Lord, "As the Lord lives, you shall incur no blame for this."

11   Then the woman asked him, "Whom do you want me to conjure up?" and he answered, "Samuel."

12   When the woman saw Samuel, she shrieked at the top of her voice and said to Saul, "Why have you deceived me? You are Saul."

13   But the king said to her, "Have no fear. What do you see?" The woman answered Saul, "I see a preternatural being rising from the earth."

14   "What does he look like?" asked Saul. And she replied, "It is an old man who is rising, clothed in a mantle." Saul knew that it was Samuel, and so he bowed face to the ground in homage.

15   Samuel then said to Saul, "Why do you disturb me by conjuring me up?" Saul replied, "I am in great straits, for the Philistines are waging war against me and God has abandoned me. Since he no longer answers me through prophets or in dreams, I have called you to tell me what I should do."

16   To this Samuel said: "But why do you ask me, if the Lord has abandoned you and is with your neighbor?

17   The Lord has done to you what he foretold through me: he has torn the kingdom from your grasp and has given it to your neighbor David.

18   Because you disobeyed the Lord's directive and would not carry out his fierce anger against Amalek, the Lord has done this to you today.

19   Moreover, the Lord will deliver Israel, and you as well, into the clutches of the Philistines. By tomorrow you and your sons will be with me, and the Lord will have delivered the army of Israel into the hands of the Philistines."

20   Immediately Saul fell full length on the ground, for he was

badly shaken by Samuel's message. Moreover, he had no bodily strength left, since he had eaten nothing all that day and night.

21 Then the woman came to Saul, and seeing that he was quite terror-stricken, said to him: "Remember, your maid-servant obeyed you; I took my life in my hands and ful-filled the request you made of me.

22 Now you, in turn, please listen to your maidservant. Let me set something before you to eat, so that you may have strength when you go on your way."

23 But he refused, saying, "I will not eat." However, when his servants joined the woman in urging him, he listened to their entreaties, got up from the ground and sat on a couch.

24 The woman had a stall-fed calf in the house, which she now quickly slaughtered. Then taking flour, she kneaded it and baked unleavened bread.

25 She set the meal before Saul and his servants, and they ate. Then they stood up and left the same night.

Mainline scholarship would agree that this is a type story, not a reportorial account. The ancient tradition knew that Saul had come to a bad end. Centuries later some author with a brilliant imagination used the conventional form of a ghost story to attempt to explain the meaning of that tradition as it fitted into Israel's ill-fated experiment with monarchy. God had been on both sides—both for the monarchy and against it. The hope of the future was also both pro and con concerning a messianic king. Just how should one understand this needed testing?[14]

Our historical reconstruction of the reign of Saul would probably picture him as a political genius who shaped the future of the monarchy decisively. He took twelve tribes which had little in common and shaped them into something like a state. He managed to preserve enough of the old egalitarian liberties of tribal life to satisfy the people and yet fashioned a central authority which was new. He gave government a place and a function in daily life throughout the area. He established a standing army and something of a judicial system which was not simply personalized in the judge. He at least recognized the possibility of the separation of powers between king, priest and prophet. Symbolically, he gave Israel a flag.

The most immediate reading of a moral into the story would be that sin is always punished. That has been the standard interpretation of the Deuteronomist's retribution theology. However, it has always been recognized by perceptive commentators that the Deuteronomist is far more sophisticated in his thinking than simply a prophet of doom. He may have been trying to confound the whole view.[15]

It is the details, realistic and unrealistic, of the story which call into question the "obvious" interpretation. First of all, the story begins with what seems irrelevant and perhaps out of character. David is planning to fight against his own people. He is so loyal to the Philistine chief that he gets the job of royal bodyguard. Nothing is said of his fidelity to Yahweh or Israel. Saul, however, is still loyal to his responsibilities as king, even when he feels that he is doomed to defeat. At the last, he confesses that he has no confidence in his army. He must seek the help of Yahweh. That is his final motivation.

However, he cannot get an answer by usual means and so he breaks his own imposed ban on witchcraft and consults a medium. The calling up of old, wrathful Samuel is depicted with considerable dramatic force by the author, and this gives him the opportunity to put into Samuel's mouth a lecture straight from the retribution theology. All the penalties, however, are earth-bound. After tomorrow, Samuel and Saul will be united in death. Nothing more is said than that they will be together. And then there is the final brilliant touch of the woman cooking a meal for Saul and his men. It is quite unrealistic and quite unnecessary for the theological point of retribution. But it does emphasize the dramatic point that tragedy should stir up pity, not condemnation.

The story thus understood may seem disappointing for studying moral decisions. It would be simpler to revert back to the fundamentalist position of saying that the moral is: sin is always punished. But it is noteworthy that this point is precisely the one which is not made in the story. The Deuteronomist was not slow in passing such judgments on the kings of Israel and Judah—he evaluated each of them on the point of sinfulness. Samuel does, indeed, condemn Saul quite clearly from that viewpoint. But does the author agree with his character of Samuel? He has surrounded his traditionalist speech with compromising details.

Several things should be noted before we pass from the story.

1. The problem is presented precisely as a story. The author, presumably, could have written an essay or at least an editorial comment as he did elsewhere. But he chose to tell a story in which he could deal with this matter by using images and simply leave it there for the reader to decipher.
2. The story is about one man, but it is set in a larger context of the monarchy. The woman of Endor addresses Saul as the king of Israel and knows the power of his royal decrees. The story was told not to govern personal actions in future times but to explain the community understanding of the ill-fated experiment with monarchy which Israel had attempted and which it was always tempted to revert to.
3. No moral judgment is made upon Saul at the end. The story which follows eventually chronicled that Saul was slain by the Philistines. Everybody knew that, and it could not be avoided. But the final judgment on Saul was not included in this story.

4. Understanding the story demands faith in Yahweh on the part both of the actors and of the readers. If Saul did not believe that his kingship depended on a power greater than himself, then there was no point at all in his consulting the witch of Endor. If the reader does not believe in such a power then the story has no reality. It is merely another entertaining ghost story.

5. If one does believe, then it is also a ghost story, but a true one insofar as it reflects the reality of human motivations and judgments within the context of supernatural powers. It ends in an act of belief. That had been the real problem with the monarchy from the beginning and into the future. Did one believe that a more effective government could provide security and prosperity, or did one believe that Yahweh would grant these blessings? Did one act as a resourceful pagan or a powerless believer?

3

Images

"OK, Smith, don't get huffy with me. I only asked if you would consider it," Higgins said.

"I don't believe in guns," Smith said calmly. "Teaches kids the wrong thing."

"That's nonsense," said Higgins. "You've got a constitutional right to bear arms. Are you going to stand up for it or not? Just give me one good reason why you wouldn't consider joining the National Rifle Association."

"The Bible," Smith said as flatly and finally as he could.

"What's the Bible got to do with it?" Higgins sputtered. "You've got more blood and guts in the Bible than anywhere else. Tell your kid not to read the Bible. They didn't use guns, of course, but they sure knew how to use swords. Give me something better than that."

"OK," said Smith. "Maybe you're right. But let me level with you. I was a cop and I knew guns. I was in Vietnam and I know about that. First you get trained in knowing how to use the gun; then you shoot at fixed targets, then at pop-up targets, and one day the pop-up target happens to be a human being. Then it's too late. You have to shoot because you have been trained that way."

"Have it your own way," Higgins sighed. "Then your kid

will grow up to be a wimp who never knew what a real gun is. All that pop-pop stuff which kids do in their imagination, but never the real thing."

This little incident was actually suggested by one of my students from his own experience. The point is not a denunciation of the NRA nor an endorsement. It simply brings to light the hidden agendas in our strongest convictions. They are not usually matters of principle, as we so righteously claim, but a mosaic of images.

Most of our decisions are made on the basis of images. The observation arises from common experience. In an extreme example most murders are not the exquisitely fashioned plots of a coldly logical mind. They are crimes of passion, committed on the spur of the moment over some domestic quarrel, provoked by some crisis of images of wrongs. Such are our crime statistics. Some years ago an experiment was made in mediating disputes between employees. The technique was to get the angry contestants to tape individually their version of the incident. Then the disputants were set down together and made to listen to both tapes. They could not interrupt, as they would have done in an argument; they had to listen for once. What they heard was not the logic they thought was in the argument, but the image which each created. Many of them said, "I didn't know that I sounded like that." Indeed, most such quarrels between people are not based essentially on the facts or logic, but on the self-images which they are defending.

Oscar Wilde wrote the memorable story of *The Picture of Dorian Gray*. Dorian Gray's portrait aged while he stayed the same, and the portrait revealed his growing viciousness. Oddly enough, Wilde seemed to be hiding his own self behind the picture. It was not "all done with mirrors," but it was an almost reluctant moral tract told in images.[1] Certainly some of our moral decisions are based on principles and conclusions;

some crimes are "in cold blood" and some of our noble deeds
are deliberately thought out. The contention here is simply
that in the press of circumstances most decisions are more or
less spontaneous and depend on images rather than logic.
Then we tell about them in stories.

The literary presentation of decisions based on images
can be discovered almost anywhere in the Bible. In the preliminaries to the story of Saul the people had demanded: "Appoint
a king over us, as other nations have, to judge us" (1 Sam 8:5).
The demand came not from some well-thought-out political
philosophy. The people simply wanted a king as the other
nations had. That was something they could see.

Proverbs 30:1b–4 has a marvelous discourse on the mystery of wisdom. Agur says:

> The pronouncement of mortal man; "I am not God.
>   I am not God that I should prevail.
> Why, I am the most stupid of men,
>   and have not even human intelligence;
> Neither have I learned wisdom,
>   nor have I the knowledge of the Holy One.
> Who has gone up to heaven and come down again—
>   who has cupped the wind in his hands?
> Who has bound up the waters in a cloak—
>   who has marked out all the ends of the earth?
> What is his name, what is his son's name,
>   if you know it?"

The whole appeal to wisdom here depends on understanding
the ineffable distance between the images of God and the
author. Jesus used the saying as the clincher in his discussion
with Nicodemus (Jn 3:13).

The author of Lamentations bases his appeal for hope on
vividly contrasting images of God.

He pierces my sides
    with shafts from his quiver.
I have become a laughingstock for all nations,
    their taunt all the day long.
He has sated me with bitter food,
    made me drink my fill of wormwood.
He has broken my teeth with gravel,
    pressed my face in the dust;
My soul is deprived of peace,
    I have forgotten what happiness is;
I tell myself my future is lost,
    all that I hoped for from the Lord.
The thought of my homeless poverty
    is wormwood and gall;
Remembering it over and over
    leaves my soul downcast within me.
But I will call this to mind,
    as my reason to have hope;
The favors of the Lord are not exhausted,
    his mercies are not spent.
They are renewed each morning,
    so great is his faithfulness.
My portion is the Lord, says my soul;
    therefore will I hope in him (Lam 3:13–24).

Every line of this poem conjures up new images which we can see and savor even while we are crying over the message itself. Paul exhorted his Christians to "be imitators of me" (Phil 3:17; cf. also 1 Cor 4:16; 11:1). That is about as direct an appeal as one can make for decision-making on images. The images do not tell us specifically what we should do, but they have a powerful effect on our actual decisions. Logic is certainly not a dominant factor.

    The psychological level of this dependence on images is fairly well understood. Psychological self-images are almost a fetish of popular psychology today. We are inclined to attribute so many human problems to "a poor self-image" and the self-help books keep encouraging us to create a positive self-image. There is enough truth in it to compel attention. The difficulty is in being honest about it.

Historical critics of the Bible have sometimes evaluated a dynamic interpretation of images as akin to malpractice. Emil Kraeling, who was a respected historical critic, wrote a novel about Paul. [2] Kraeling was considered somewhat out of bounds by the academic community although it was generally judged that he had stuck to the facts insofar as the facts are relevant in such an enterprise. However, psychoanalyzing characters is not ordinarily permitted in historical biblical criticism. On the other hand, a novelist or dramatist cannot set about his work without having a clear idea of the image of his characters. Eventually, most biblical critics are tempted to cross the line between presumed objectivity and the need for pictures. Paul is an attractive subject since so many of his emotions are revealed in his letters. Much analysis of Paul's ethical stances turns out to be largely a character study. This is very revealing.

For example, most critics presume that Paul changed his view of the second coming of Christ from a short time to a long-delayed prospect. No compelling historical data is adduced for this view, and a need is felt to explain the change by a psychological reason in Paul's personal self-understanding. On the grounds of the method being used, there is no justification for this but the temptation to do so is very strong. What is happening seems to be as much related to the self-image of the commentator as to that of the biblical character.

Occasionally some one will write a book, such as *The Passover Plot*, or make a movie, such as *The Last Temptation of Christ*, which will trigger popular denunciation. Sometimes that reaction is justified and sometimes not. The point here is simply that there is a clash between what someone is proposing as a true picture of Christ and what the readers or viewers hold to be the real Christ. Then accusations of "blasphemy" or "dishonesty" or "superficiality" fly. The battle is not really fought over principles, but over the images. In any case, it becomes a moral problem.

In biblical interpretation the conflict often arises out of a matching of pre-conceived images which we hold today with what is claimed to be the proper image in the biblical text. Obviously, there is a reality somewhere in these conflicting images, and we need to deal with it in our interpretation of moral norms in the Bible, if such they be. "Why do you notice the splinter in your brother's eye, but do not perceive the wooden beam in your own eye?" (Mt 7:3). The little saying is aware of how self-images can distort. James says: "If anyone is a hearer of the word and not a doer, he is like a man who looks at his own face in a mirror. He sees himself, then goes off and promptly forgets what he looked like" (Jas 1:23–24). Most of us instinctively look the other way. The point here is that one needs to be aware of the psychological factor both in the biblical text and in oneself.

The effect of images extends also both to the society in which the biblical action is taking place and to ourselves. In the conflict with the Jews in John 8:31–41 Jesus says: " 'If you remain in my word, you will truly be my disciples, and you will know the truth, and the truth will set you free.' They answered him, 'We are descendants of Abraham and have never been enslaved to anyone' " (Jn 8:31–33). Their defense, so stoutly stated, is ludicrous in the light of historical facts, but that did not deter them from clinging to the self-image. Both the accusation and the defense presume psychological images of a whole group in society. We certainly misunderstand the scene and the moral accusation made by Jesus if we do not carefully search out the historical facts. But we also need to consider the psychological imaging which is involved in the discourse. Then we also need to examine our own self-understanding of what a claim by one man to equality with God actually means to us in ethical situations. We need to understand that not simply as a personal question, but as a factor within our own society and its self-image making. If we have a self-sufficient image of ourselves as a society, we don't need a Son of God.

On an ontological or more properly scientific theological level the same is perceived by ethicists. Richard McCormick, one of our most distinguished Catholic ethicists, has termed this factor "pre-discursive understanding" in moral decision-making. Karl Rahner, the great theologian, in his theory of "categorical acts" speaks of those daily acts which flow almost unnoticed from a "transcendental act" of total surrender to God.[3] Joseph Fuchs, who has dominated European Catholic ethics for years, follows Rahner. Both are redefining human nature in terms of natural law. The image presented by the traditional "rational animal" must be made more concrete and real. Within Protestant circles greater emphasis has been put of late on biblical ethics as a question of "formation of character."[4]

What we are doing here is redefining our definition of the moral agent. The traditional Catholic definition was Aristotelian: rational animal. It is more complex than that when we come down to the individual agent and the specific act. In Christian decision making the process begins with a commitment in faith; that cannot be explained rationally. We shall come back to this later.

THE TIMELESSNESS OF IMAGES

In 608 B.C. the prophet Jeremiah was formally accused of treason for predicting that Jerusalem would become as forgotten and desolate as Shiloh. The penalty sought was death. The accusation was brought by the priests and cultic prophets who were threatened by such a prediction; they and some disgruntled government officials could not stand criticism. The princes and the people, however, were more fair-minded and wanted to hear Jeremiah himself. He reminded them that he had spoken only what the Lord had told him. Jeremiah convinced the princes, but the priests and prophets were adamant. Finally some of the elders of the land came forth and said:

> Micah of Moresheth used to prophesy in the days of Hezekiah, king of Judah, and he told all the people of Judah: Thus says the Lord of hosts:
>
> > Zion shall become a plowed field,
> > Jerusalem a heap of ruins
> > and the temple mount a forest ridge.
>
> Did Hezekiah, king of Judah, and all Judah condemn him to death? Did they not rather fear the Lord and entreat the favor of the Lord, so that he repented of the evil which he had threatened them? But we are on the point of committing this great evil to our own undoing (Jer 26:18–19).

The elders of the land are proposing a moral decision on the basis of images remembered from a century before. We would probably talk about freedom of speech in such circumstances, but that is an abstraction and does not have the punch of the story of Micah. The common people still remembered the words of Micah of Moresheth; few of us remember who originated the phrase "freedom of speech."

In a way this is "exemplar morality" and it certainly has its value. Christ used it in the incident of his disciples plucking grain on the sabbath to feed themselves. In Mark 2:25–26 he says: "Have you never read what David did when he was in need and he and his companions were hungry? How he en-

tered into the house of God when Abiathar was high priest
and ate the bread of offering that only the priests could law-
fully eat, and shared it with his companions?" In these and
numerous other biblical passages a previous example is cited as
a parallel for present action. Jeremiah is equated to Micah,
Jesus to David, image to image.

Obviously, there are great dangers of over-simplification
in such a process. Israelis are accustomed to cite the example
of father Abraham owning the whole of Palestine to justify
present day claims. Fundamentalists of all kinds endlessly find
justification in so-called examples. Both war and peace can be
equally and emphatically defended on this basis without much
thought.[5]

GETTING FROM THEN TO NOW

We need to use all the available critical helps available.
Advocacy of a rhetorical approach does not negate or disre-
gard the invaluable contributions of historical criticism or indeed of any of the commonly accepted critical methods. Sociological criticism is particularly helpful for us in assessing the
effects which any particular rhetorical presentation might
have had on the original audience. When Ahaz in 725 B.C.
refused to accept a sign from the Lord that Judah would be
preserved, we need to understand as much as we can about the
politics (Is 7). We also need to understand what impact that
virgin-birth prophecy would have had in the society in which
it was pronounced. Obviously, we also need to understand as
accurately as possible the original text and its meaning of the
words.

The real problem is in getting the ancient images to apply
to the particular circumstances in which we as individuals
presently exist. The *then* and the *now* is the real nub of any

problem about application of the Bible to current moral problems. This has been recognized by the better commentators in all ages, but it tends to be overlooked by many who do not ask how they got from there to here.

Rudolf Bultmann, the principal author of form criticism of the New Testament, was really seeking for a way to do this. His contemporary Dibelius was even more concerned. Dibelius had been a chaplain in the German army during World War I. He found that his soldier audience was not really interested in his preaching about theological dogmas. That did not speak their language nor appeal to their images of life.

Both Dibelius and Bultmann adopted an approach called "demythologizing" and "remythologizing." "Demythologizing" meant analyzing biblical stories within the stream of mythology with which we humans have endlessly watered our dreams of explaining God and ourselves. There is a great deal of such information available from worldwide sources, and there are similarities among them all.[6] The hero stories with their dying and rising gods, their journeys in search of immortality, and their sufferings, etc. are universal themes which express our struggles with reality and our hopes for nobility. The proposal of Bultmann and Dibelius was that if the kernel of biblical stories could be isolated as myths in this sense, then we should be able to transform those themes into contemporary pictures which would appeal to moderns. Science fiction tries to do this. This approach is basically through comparative mythology. It spans the ages by timeless stories about the gods.

Unfortunately, scholars who adopted form criticism became more interested in the mechanics of forms and the historical setting than in the "demythologizing." The ultimate aim of "remythologizing" seems to have been almost completely lost in scholarly study of the Bible. Perhaps the present dissatisfaction with historical criticism is due most of all to that failure.

We are left with only a vague ability to say: "Well, now, there is something like that in our present situation." But we do not really understand how to draw the parallels or to control the application to get from there to here.

Actually, we are subjective. The methods we use are different from the methods which the fathers of the third and fourth century used; they are different from those of the medieval scholastics and from the methods of the renaissance and the Protestant reformers. For Catholics they are even different from those which were used prior to 1950. No one can say whether the contemporary methods are better or worse than those which our ancestors used. They appeal to us because they are congenial to the spirit of our age. We have stressed that they are "scientific," and that is spontaneously accepted as better. But as our confidence in science has eroded since World War II, our confidence in "scientific" methods of biblical interpretation has also lessened. Literary or rhetorical methods of interpretation are again being espoused as more humane and realistic in our world. Methods do not give us timeless and objective standards; they simply put some control on our present, subjective seeking.

Great literature is also a means of tapping the enduring flow of great ideas from age to age and culture to culture. Literature does have some universal techniques and consistencies. There are, after all, a limited number of plots which can be used for story-telling. The enumeration of such stories in ancient literature has been rather thoroughly explored. We have all heard the saying that there are only five (or some such number) original jokes. The same can be said about the great stories we canonize as literature.

The stories of the savior gods—Joseph Campbell called them "The Hero with a Thousand Faces"—continue even though we are often not aware of them in our technical society.[7] The basic myth involves a journey from some previous place into the unknown, then combat with horrendous forces, a departure which is often the departure from life itself and an arrival at a new birth. It is found in the oldest myths we know and in the myths of the "dying and rising gods" which have sometimes been adduced as the source for the New Testament drama. It is found even in the classic western novel of our culture—the "good guy" who rides into a town which the "bad guys" have taken over, leads to a combat with the "bad guys" and ends with "The Shootout at the OK Corral" or some such, and then the hero vanishes "as the sun is setting slowly in the west." Joseph Campbell toward the end of his life was fascinated by science-fiction and served as an advisor for the movie "Star Wars." He found that movie to be an echo of the original savior myth. These are all ethical tales. Good order always prevails in the end.

That the Bible has evidences of such patterns simply means that the Bible is realistic in understanding that this is the way human beings communicate with one another. What is different about the Bible is that so often the myth pattern contradicts or transcends the normal pattern. That is the focal point of its revelation. It is not the seven days of creation in an ordered sequence which is unusual—that can be found all over the mythical landscape; it is the upsetting saying: "And God said: Let us make man in our own image, after our likeness." That is truly different.

I shall simply note here that poetry and instruction, which make up a large part of the biblical tradition which bears on ethics, also have their typical ways of communicating. To get these into our ethical outlook we must look at the problem primarily as one of communication more than logic, and we must realize that we are involved in an art more than a science.

Patterns such as this, whether of mythology or more ordinary story-telling, whether of poetry or clan wisdom, are embedded in our social traditions. We are not born in a vacuum; our mind-set is already fixed by the parents we had, the education we received, the religion to which we belong, the society in which we operate, the particular set of peers among whom we have been set down, the literary traditions of our society and our own particular aptitudes—plus a good number of unknowns.

We are inclined to use the computer as a metaphor. As I type this manuscript on a word processor and a program called WordPerfect, I have available a key which is called "Reveal Codes." When the computer does something which I do not want, I press Reveal Codes and it tells me what some of the hidden codes embedded in the program are doing. There are many more codes hidden in the program which I never see but which turn my decisions to strike a particular key into something that makes sense. Similarly, we have these hidden codes in our social make-up. They come from many influences—our family, our education, our culture, our tastes, and, especially in moral matters, our religious heritage. They tend to make our decisions for us.

But here the computer analogy breaks down. Mysteriously, we are not programmed to respond in a logical and necessary way as the computer is. We are free and we put things together in a creative manner which does not always follow rules.

Mostly, this is a literary or rhetorical problem, and the problem revolves largely around images. In rhetoric the ancients discovered *inventio*. *Inventio* means simply finding the right way to get into the subject. We all know that from advertising and speech-making. The beginning is all important; it must present the right picture, the right story, the right phrase for establishing rapport. Counseling is like that too. The first words, whether of commendation or blame, determine much of what will follow. What is the image that is created?

Some images move some people but do not affect others; some move us at one time and not at others. We are all aware of how at various times certain sentences or phrases leap out of a text at us. Some music, some poetry, some oratory, even some new sight may inspire us—and we do not know why. Such experiences seem to open up new vistas of insight which we have never had before, and we may live for days in the glow of that illumination. In time they fade and are replaced by others.

Ontologically, the medieval philosophers also called this process "illumination," an imaged word. They spoke of the natural light of reason and also of the supernatural light of grace. Our society does not believe very much in the supernatural light. We have difficulty even sitting still long enough to savor a text peacefully until it does illumine our minds in some way; we do not really expect God to have much to do with it.

What we are talking about is the art of communication between God and us and between ourselves. Biblical criticism as well as the older philosophy tried to reduce it to a science. Historical criticism has been bedeviled by unexplainable flexibilities in the way in which the biblical authors wrote. In the psalms historical criticism has made a notable effort to classify these poems by categories which have a precise and repeated form. We have a minute catalogue. Unfortunately, the majority of psalms do not follow the rules. Yet the poetry often gets to us in spite of the lack of formalities. The same is true of form-criticism in the New Testament. The gospels have an underlying freedom of expression which will not allow us to develop rules and objective modes of interpretation which are always certain guides. There is an art to the production of the images as they exist in the ancient text and there is an art in ourselves to developing the images by which we live. Obviously, to connect the two is itself an art.

To accomplish this the commentator—in this case, the ethicist—must have experienced problems personally. In some way the scholar is always subjectively involved. The moralist who ponders a case in his study can be totally dissociated from the individuals involved. Yet he is giving a decision which affects their lives and which affects his personal character and reputation. Whether he is an honest workman or a charlatan is very much the question. For that he is morally responsible. On the other hand, the decision-maker must be far enough removed from the unconscious images to be able to dig them out and make an honest estimate of their authenticity. Many of our self-images are mirages. We must have the honesty and insight to be able to sift through them. Any method of interpretation is a circle.[8] We start with something; we look for meaning and eventually we come back to applying the meaning to the something we started with. The interpreter must know the point on the hermeneutical circle from which the procedure starts and where it stops.[9]

THE IMAGE CONVEYOR

The process of self-argumentation is often unconscious. "Good shepherd," "good Samaritan," "the rich man and Lazarus," "the vine and the branches," "Adam and Eve," etc.—the biblical images in our cultural background are endless and pop up spontaneously. It does not matter that most people have never seen a shepherd; certainly, they know nothing of how to shepherd. Where Samaria may be doesn't matter; the portrait of the good Samaritan is part of the language and the culture. Other phrases may be less familiar depending on one's religious heritage. Some are dependent on one's personal experience. However, they are all conveyed by the literature and culture in which they are embedded and they get us thinking.

This is the most obvious connection between "then" and "now." It happens in all good literature. The literature is a creation of the culture, but in its turn the literature is a transmitter and recreator of the culture. Moreover, good stories transfer easily from one age and one culture to another. Grimm's Fairy Tales are exportable to anywhere. Children's stories show a great ability to leap from nation to nation and from century to century. The Germans esteem Shakespeare almost as much as the English; most of us at least know about Dante's "Divina Commedia." The forms of story-telling—hero, tragedy, comedy—seem to be common to all languages.

Below the level of the events of the story we encounter myth. Myth is the story-telling version of theology. It is the search for the gods and for our place in the universe. Why these stories have such commonality among so many people, we do not know; we do know from comparative religion that the similarities exist.[10] Myths, such as creation stories, have no evidence in fact, yet it seems almost imperative for the human mind to create a story of beginnings.

The philosopher would say that certain patterns of communication exist in the human mind and that language must appeal to them for communication. Such is the basic thesis of structuralism.[11] It begins with a philosophical conviction that such innate patterns do exist and are independent of specific languages. Languages all have the same basic structures; they differ only in how we vocalize them. Reading a written text, then, is a philosophical exercise in unearthing these hidden structures of language. Scarcely anybody would think of this in making a moral decision, and the theory may be totally wrong. Yet it exists as a conviction which the Greeks first expressed: the word does depend on something independent of our thinking it.

This does affect how we make decisions. The relations of

men and women do depend on respect; sexual discrimination begins with a false idea of who the other sex is. So we use titles of respect for one another. Does the dignity and the difference of the sexes exist apart from language or respect? Is it simply nice words or is there something real there? The book of Proverbs is noted for its beautiful hymns to Lady Wisdom. Lady Wisdom is the opposite of her shadow, the Stranger Woman. Much scholarly research has been devoted to pursuing the myth of Wisdom through comparative literature of the Ancient Near East—and much does exist from Ma'at of the Egyptians to the seven sisters of the Mesopotamians. But is this the proper way to go about motivating people to be egalitarian about the sexes? Is it just a literary confection? Or did Lady Wisdom exist before the word? Do we begin with a concept, give it a female form and call it a personification? Or do we begin with a reality and discover that it already exists in the good wife?

Similarly, is the Word of God an abstraction to which we give a name and a human face, Jesus? Or is the Word of God a reality which exists both before the language tag and in some real person? And if the latter options are true, how must we then respect the individual person? These are truly moral questions which we ask daily, and we already have some preconceived notions about them. Many of them are likely to be pre-conceived on what we have heard from the Bible. The trans-temporal and trans-cultural jump has taken place even in our philosophical theories.

There is another transmitter of interpretation called tradition. The recent resurgence of canonical criticism has once again directed attention to the role which the church has played in the interpretation of the Bible. What has been preserved has been a canonical text, a sacred book which cannot be changed. The book was canonized precisely to keep it from changing. But this affected not only the text in itself, but also the interpretation. More will be said about this later.

Some rhetoricians believe that any text is open to an endless variety of meanings. If two of us see a movie and you get one idea out of it and I get another, who will say that you are wrong and I am right? The story may have a multiplicity of interpretations; canons of dramatic style do impose some limitations—which is why we have critics—but do not dictate. Historical criticism by itself seems to limit meaning to historical facts, but the experience of historical criticism has been that scholars often do not agree in their conclusions. In fact, some of their most insightful conclusions about the aesthetics of biblical passages seem to be totally irrelevant to the method they have used.

Most of the basic tenets which Christians hold are specific interpretations of individual texts which may be interpreted in different ways. The incarnation, the Trinity, the virgin birth, the eucharist, the nature of the church, etc. are all dependent on texts whose meaning could go one way or the other. Yet sometimes the text was canonized within a tradition which at a particular time said that this is what the text means—perhaps not the only thing, but certainly this.

The matter is clearest in doctrinal definitions. The Catholic Church has never defined *de fide* any specific moral decisions nor even the basis for moral decisions, such as declaring that the natural law is a teaching which must be held by all. Obviously, it has taught with less than such final conclusiveness many things about the family, the state, the church, the economy, etc. But it has not defined *de fide* any of these things. In our age it can be firmly against abortion, war, homosexuality, slave wages, and many other things. The authority gets diluted as these run down to more specifics. But there is no doubt that the church tradition does put some limit on the meanings which we may assign to biblical texts. The Council of Trent was one of our few attempts to tie down doctrines to specific texts. Undoubtedly, the texts do mean what that council said. As a Catholic I accept that. They may also mean other things, but they do mean what the council said.

In theological language we are talking about *sensus fidelium* and *magisterium*. *Sensus fidelium* ("the sense of the faithful") means the proper understanding of Christians everywhere and at all times. There can be only a rough estimate of true understanding, but it still remains the final criterion of infallibility.[12] The *magisterium* ("teaching authority") is the verbalizing of such teaching by various officials of the church. The church is the teacher both in its faithful and in its hierarchy, who are also the faithful. Such is the tradition. It is not a very logical tradition, but tradition is not based on logic. That is not the meaning of the word.[13]

These are abstractions, but we know them more immediately in our common experience. "I am the good shepherd, and I know mine and mine know me" (Jn 10:14). Many interpretations can be given to that comparison, most of them not very flattering to the sheep. One may see here paternalism run riot. Or cynicism. But that is not the way our religious—and literary—interpretation has canonized the text. "If your right hand causes you to sin, cut it off and throw it away" (Mt 5:30). That is absurd and surely not a moral norm, although some ancient Christians attempted to follow it literally. But the tradition has interpreted that saying in a generic and spiritual way and that is the way we accept it. I am not saying that these are absolutes; it is tradition with a small "t." In evaluating our images for moral decision-making we must pay attention to the tradition. We usually live in only one tradition; if we ignore it, we ostracize ourselves from others and cannot communicate. Hence it has been said often enough that only a believer can interpret the Bible.

THE ART OF BEGINNING

One begins at any point on the circle of deciding. One can begin with the biblical text, perhaps by reading a Bible in a motel or listening to a sermon. Not too many people nowadays read the Bible on a regular basis. Sermons and radio talks are probably closer to our point of contact. At any rate, we hear something which sets us to thinking about a moral problem which we have. The train of thought begins to involve all those images which have come out of our whole milieu of family, education, society, peers, personal dispositions, church affiliation, etc. as noted above. We sift and sort and fit the pieces together into some pattern which satisfies us. Normally we do not recreate a great synthesis of all our moral beliefs; our specific decision may be contrary to a good number of other beliefs. Andrew Greeley has remarked in his sociological studies of post-Vatican II Catholics in the United States that they sometimes seem to have managed to combine loyalty to the cult of the Catholic Church with disagreement about its teachings on sexual morality, war, economics, etc. One does not look for much logic or conscious method in our ordinary moral discourse with ourselves.

On the other hand, one may begin on the opposite side of the circle, namely, the present situation. We have a problem and we worry it with emotions and plots. A somewhat organized solution may emerge from logical conclusion to instinct. Then one may search the scriptures for collaboration, correction or further insight. Scholars are inclined to do this since they know so much about the biblical text and can with relative ease locate where they presume that their convictions came from. One may consult a biblical "armory," one of those old books which refer to passages in the scriptures according to topic. Or, as often is the case with fundamentalists, one may have a store of such proof-texts within the tradition itself and all one needs to do is to tap into memory. Our older Catholic moralists were inclined to do something like this by "proof-texts."

The writers of the New Testament quote the previous sacred scriptures frequently. Isaiah and the psalms are favorites. There is a theory that the early Christians used a kind of handbook of proof-texts for illustrating the real character of Jesus. We do not know this for sure, but there is a similarity in the way in which they quote favorite passages. At any rate, they never seem to be at a loss to find an appropriate opening for their thoughts in the older scriptures. Paul bases the whole of his essay to the Romans on a quote from the prophet Habakkuk, "The one who is righteous by faith shall live" (Rom 1:17). The rest of the epistle is a commentary on that verse. John's gospel begins with the great prologue which is obviously modeled on the first chapter of Genesis: "In the beginning was the Word and the Word was with God and the Word was God" (Jn 1:1). The pattern is clear, but there is more to it than just the pattern. The "Word" is a traditional term, identified both with Wisdom and with the Torah. In the religious tradition both were mysterious realities which somehow had a pre-existence.

Matthew begins his gospel with an infancy narrative which is based on the story of Joseph in Egypt and then mingles in references to the story of Moses.[14] The opening point is artistically framed around a tradition. The previous stories are not repeated; a phrase or a sentence manages to conjure up the whole story which is merely alluded to. These are not logical proofs; they are persuasive appeals to a tradition. Sometimes the appeal is to images which have become symbols and have a whole wealth of meaning. "Sheep," "vines," "wine," "bread," "seed," "Jerusalem," etc. need only be mentioned to strike a well-ornamented host of meanings. This is true artistry, often very creative. Matthew concludes his infancy narrative at the return to Nazareth by: "so that what had been spoken through the prophets might be fulfilled, 'He shall be called a Nazorean' "

(Mt 2:23). There is no such text in any of the prophets. Yet the citation truly captures something of what was in the tradition.

The great need here is for control. However, since we are talking about literature, not about science, the control must be a literary one. What is appropriate and fitting can be determined only by a literary critique; what the significance of the *inventio* or selection of the biblical passage may be must be determined similarly. The texts referred to above seem to have little to do with morals, although they do fit in. In more directly moral connotations we need to understand the *inventio* clearly. Paul exhorts the Corinthians to beware of associating with people who do not believe in the resurrection of the dead. "Bad company corrupts good morals," he says (1 Cor 15:33). It is probably a free quote from popular proverbs and certainly not religious. It is an observation of common sense, not a moral rule. Yet it does have a moral implication. He applies it by continuing, "Become sober as you ought and stop sinning" (1 Cor 15:34). The possible sin is one against faith and that is the most important moral act of all. As Paul said: "If the dead are not raised, 'Let us eat and drink, for tomorrow we die!' " (1 Cor 15:32b). Paul is not using a proof-text; he is illustrating his whole attitude by taking off from a well-known quotation in the book of Ecclesiastes and a proclamation of faith.

What appeals to us as fitting depends on the whole complex of experiences we have had. We see these things as images. Not only are these different for each individual; they vary from day to day. For the process to happen—and we are simply documenting what does happen—there must be a dialogue between the text and the decision-maker. Some references are rejected because we have not had that kind of experience; some are rejected because we have prejudices, and some strike home because we already believe. The best are the ones which set us to thinking anew. This is the artistry of our initial step in making decisions which are based on the Bible.

4

Conflict

There is no good story without conflict. A fairy tale ends: "And they lived happily ever after." No more can be said since two people living happily ever after is a deadly dull plot. In the simplest hero stories we always have the "guys with the white hats" and the "guys with the black hats." Tragedies are, of course, contests between the forces of good and evil. Comedy always begins with a conflict or problem of some sort; it is the resolution which is ironic or paradoxical. The worth of a story depends on how deeply one has penetrated into the conflict and how realistically one has depicted it. Plots about mere mechanical problems may be interesting as information but they do not make for great literature. The real problems are between those mysterious and other-earthly forces of good and evil which seize upon us. For a Catholic it has always been difficult to make a "mortal sin" out of a church law such as "no meat on Friday."

In recent years much more attention has been given to this conflict element. John's gospel is a good example. John escalates the conflict with the Jews by transposing the scene of the cleansing of the temple to the beginning of the public ministry. There is no doubt about the seriousness of the conflict. The Jews challenged Jesus: " 'What sign can you show for doing this?' Jesus answered and said to them, 'Destroy this temple and in three days I will raise it up' " (Jn 2:18–19). The reference to "this temple" seems clear enough in the setting and that is the way the audience, including the disciples, seems to have understood it.

But this is not what Jesus meant and the omniscient narrator carries the meaning to the death scene. "But he was speaking about the temple of his body" (Jn 2:21). Then he adds another editorial comment to make this even more clear. "Therefore, when he was raised from the dead, his disciples remembered that he had said this, and they came to believe the scripture and the word Jesus had spoken" (Jn 2:22). The narrator has escalated the conflict by placing it at the beginning of the ministry and then compounding it with conflicting understandings among the disciples themselves. This technique of conflict and misunderstanding is so common in John that it has become the subject of major study.[1]

The same phenomenon occurs also in the instructional material of the Bible. By "instructional" I mean the proverbs, essays, rules, sermons and epistles, etc. The primary form of such instruction seems to have been the proverb—a pithy saying derived from common observation and wisdom. Most proverbs are antitheses. An early collection in the book of Proverbs begins:

> A wise son makes his father glad,
>   but a foolish son is a grief to his mother (Prv 10:1).

The psalms sometimes enshrine this popular wisdom in song. Psalm 1, which sets the keynote for the collection, begins:

> Happy the man who follows not
>   the counsel of the wicked
> Nor walks in the way of sinners,
>   nor sits in the company of the insolent (Ps 1:1).

It ends:

> For the Lord watches over the way of the just,
>   but the way of the wicked vanishes (Ps 1:6).

Paul is a master of the art. The most common feature of his style is strong antithesis, indeed paradox. He will set code words boldly against one another.

> For God's folly is wiser than men,
>   and his weakness more powerful than men (1 Cor 1:25).[2]

The prophetic preaching is also marked with these sharp contrasts. There is no true prophet who simply prophesies doom—or salvation. The prophetic preaching is always a mixture of the two. It has become conventional for scholars to divide the book of Isaiah into the Book of Woes and the Book of Consolation. It is the whole which was the message of Isaiah, and one quotes the woes alone or the consolations alone to one's own confusion.

Apocalyptic is a special kind of literature which we will need to consider separately later. It abounds in conflicts between celestial forces whose existence we may not be aware of. It is most important for our consideration of retribution and redemption.

Since the Bible is the word of God in its totality and not simplistically in its individual verses, knowing the essence of the conflict is most important. A strong retribution outlook invades much of the Bible. One may be tempted to read it as a set of rules which must be observed under pain of hell-fire and damnation. We cannot write this out of the text except under pain of being unrealistic. That penalties flow from defiance of various violations is one of our earliest experiences. "Daddy spanks" gets the baby to act in suitable ways. The book of

Proverbs 13:24 canonizes the common wisdom: "He who spares his rod hates his son, but he who loves him takes care to chastise him." It will be noted, however, that the retribution note of this saying is essentially modified by the balancing statement "he who loves him . . ."

Both the Old Testament and the New have considerable elements of a retribution theology since that is so evidently part of our experience of life. Retribution, however, is not the point of the Bible as a whole; it is simply the matrix of the conflict. The major symbol in the Old Testament is the exodus and that is a symbol of freedom; the major symbol of the New Testament is the cross and that is a symbol of redemption. More will be said of this later.

This first consideration concerns the literary expression of conflict. John 8:2–11 is the well-known story of the woman taken in adultery. The plot is an authentic reflection of the common themes of self-righteousness, bluster and embarrassment. The scribes and Pharisees throw the woman before Christ. The storyteller makes clear that they do this simply to embarrass and trap him (Jn 8:6). Jesus avoids the trap by doodling in the dust and then turns the question on them: "Let the one among you who is without sin be the first to throw a stone at her" (Jn 8:7). At the end he refuses to pass judgment himself in contrast to those who were so willing to do so. We applaud and we feel that we know the experience. But there is more to it than that. How great was the danger to the woman? Would they have stoned her?

Forget the legalities and the historical circumstances as the key to understanding. This certainly was not a real legal trial; evidence was not legally presented; Jesus had no authority nor obligation to make a decision. Leviticus 20:10 had said: "If a man commits adultery with his neighbor's wife, both the adulterer and the adulteress shall be put to death." Apart from the fact that the law does not fit the case very well, it is

unthinkable that the law was ever used for capital punishment
in such an off-hand way.

As with so many other sayings in the Old Testament, we
are dealing in Leviticus not with a criminal code but with a
sermon which begins: "Be holy, for I, the Lord, your God, am
holy" (Lev 19:2). It was a matter of personal decision. The
scribes and Pharisees tried to use societal images of the pious
law-observer to embarrass Jesus. It was a bluff. The images
which are legitimately involved are not those of the law-and-
order believer versus the renegade, but the interpretation of
sin and the holy God.

The conflict of images in our decision-making goes even
deeper than the actions involved. At the end it is a question of
the real "me." Ethics deals with abstractions such as "moral
agent" or "nature," "character," "root of being," etc., which
are all abstract words. The Bible does not use such terms.
Sometimes an accommodation is attempted. Josef Fuchs, the
foremost Catholic ethicist at present, analyzes 1 Corinthians 7
which speaks of the duties of the married, slaves, the unmar-
ried, and widows. Fuchs sees that what is required "above all"
is for the Christian to belong to Christ. This is what defines
essential goodness. But then there are the words of the Lord
about divorce, Paul's own advice about remaining as one and
the social customs of Corinth which are "also" necessary. The
"also" is rooted in the "above all," and it is this which gives
Christian ethics its distinctive character.[3] Such is the theoretical explanation.

In this case the imaging of the reality is rather clearly
expressed. Fuchs, who is a theologian, would probably be
more comfortable with Rahner's terms: "transcendental and
categorical acts"; in fact, he frequently uses them. However,
many of our philosophical and theological terms are enshrined
in imaged words such as illumination, beatific vision, eucharist, Son of God, children of God, etc. Given the paradoxical

nature of many of our basic Christian beliefs, theologians have a tendency to escape unconsciously into rhetoric rather than logic, since rhetoric can handle such antitheses more easily.

THE CONFLICT IN THE STORY AND IN US

The crucial question is how the conflict affects us, especially when we are brought up short by some biblical text or teaching. From a literary standpoint narrative illustrates it best. We identify with characters in a story. We cry over a sad story because we feel how much we would be hurt. We laugh at a comedy as we identify with the illogical turn of events which we have experienced. We cheer on the hero and hiss the villain because we want to be the success that the hero personifies.

Occasionally the Bible gives us a glimpse of an author caught in his own situation. The book of Esther is a strong and apparently immoral tale. Haman, the pagan prime minister of King Ahasuerus, has secured a royal decree that all Jews should be executed. Mordecai, a conniving Jewish counselor, manipulates Esther, a beautiful Jewish girl who becomes queen, to have another royal decree issued which the Jews interpret as allowing them to slaughter their enemies before the pogrom can be carried out. The Jews celebrate a great victory and institute the feast of Purim to commemorate it. In later centuries when the Jews celebrated the feast of Purim they read the story aloud and sometimes the audience made a melodrama out of it by cheering on Mordecai and hissing at Haman.

The Hebrew text has been somewhat of an embarrassment in the canon. Besides its bloody theme, the Hebrew text hardly mentions God at all. Jewish commentators sometimes justify it on the basis that whatever preserves the chosen people is good in the eyes of God.[4] There is something to be said for this, but it always smacks of special pleading.

A curious thing happened when the book was translated into Greek. The editor added a number of prayers and introduced God to the readers. But he also used a creative author's technique by explaining the point he saw in the story by a dream sequence at the beginning and an explanation of the dream at the end. Mordecai's dream at the beginning is of two great dragons who threaten the whole race. Then God causes a great river to come forth which kept the dragons away and allowed the lowly to destroy the nobles who had caused it all (Est A:4–10). At the end the dream is explained. "The river is Esther. The two dragons are myself and Haman. The nations are those who assembled to destroy the name of the Jews, but my people is Israel, who cried to God and was saved" (Est F:1–6).

Now it is evident that the translator who added this has seen the significance of identifying himself with Mordecai and making a moral judgment. In one way Mordecai is a noble hero who is instrumental in fostering God's will. That was traditional teaching. In another way Mordecai has blood on his hands of his own making. That does not fit well with the tradition, but it does fit well with our experience when it is honestly perceived. There is no final verdict in the Greek additions on who was right and who was wrong in this conflict, only an insight that it was God, not Mordecai, who saved his people.

Paul also occasionally lets us in on his own personal struggles. At the end of the painful correspondence with Corinth, he takes the "spare the rod and spoil the child" approach. "I warned those who sinned earlier and all the others, and I warn them now while absent, as I did when present on my second visit, that if I come again I will not be lenient" (2 Cor 13:2). And so on. Then he suddenly switches his tone as if realizing that he was creating the wrong image for a man who always believed in personal responsibility. "Examine yourselves to see whether you are living in faith. Test yourselves. Do you not realize that Jesus Christ is in you?—unless, of course, you fail the test" (2 Cor 13:5). One can clearly see Paul's inner struggle as he changes from the stern disciplinarian who must maintain order to the man who said that he understood the mystery of redemption.

Perhaps Paul's best description of his own personal conflict is in Romans 7. "Apart from the law sin is dead. I once lived outside the law, but when the commandment came, sin became alive; then I died" (Rom 7:8b–10a). Within this one chapter Paul repeats the idea three times, so important is it to him, and we must understand it concretely.[5] Perhaps as a child he had memorized the commandments, particularly the one "Thou shalt not covet" which he cites. But then he had some experience of coveting, and the commandment which was so easy to recite threatened to kill all the joy of his life. At the end of this passage he admits that the conflict still rages within him.

In Mark 10:17–21 we have the picture of the rich young man who is enthralled with Jesus and wants to follow him. He knows what the law tells him to do. Then Jesus says: "Go, sell what you have, and give to [the] poor . . . ; then come, follow me." Mark adds the editorial comment that "his face fell, and he went away sad, for he had many possessions" (Mk 10:22). The decision was made in the midst of conflicting images. He didn't know that they existed until the Lord spoke.

SYSTEM OR EXPERIENCE?

It is these literary presentations of conflict in the Bible which make it so difficult to erect a logical synthesis of either doctrine or morals. The stories are not all soothingly good. David is a hero but also a villain in many ways. Jesus is the

gentle and compassionate friend of sinners; he is also the fierc-
est critic of sinners. It is not only the willfully wrong, such as
the scribes and Pharisees whom he denounces unmercifully,
but also his own followers whose little faith is cause for many
admonitions.

When we try to put together all that is in the Bible by
uniting the tradition in various themes such as love, or freedom or covenant, or presence, we find that it never fits perfectly.[6] There is too much threat to allow love to dominate;
there is too much love to allow punishment to be the theme.
Freedom and the obligations of the common life clash in Paul.
It is admitted that each of the four gospels depicts Jesus in a
different way and that there is no way to harmonize all four.
We have given up talking about a theology of the Bible and are
content to talk of theologies. That is the way we perceive life
to be.

The authors themselves seem totally disinterested in trying to make this all come out even. In the proverbial and
prophetic preaching the contrasts and paradoxes are so appar-
ent that no one can doubt that the authors were aware of them.
Qoheleth, who casts himself as a wise man, mocks the very
proverbial wisdom which he is espousing. In 7:1 he says (and
see the following verses):

> A good name is better than good ointment,
>   and the day of death than the day of birth.

As a matter of fact, Qoheleth doesn't seem to think that there
is any explanation for human life. In the marvelous poem
about "there is a time for everything under heaven" (Eccl 3:1–
8) he simply assumes the inevitability of everything that happens, right or wrong. He assumes also that God controls everything, but he has no idea of how. "He has made everything
appropriate to its time, and has put the timeless into their

hearts, without men's ever discovering, from beginning to end, the work which God has done" (Eccl 3:11). This rather defies any moral system since we don't know where it all ends. The theme of so much of this practical wisdom is stated often enough: "The fear of the Lord is the beginning of knowledge" (Prv 1:7). Plain awe keeps us from a simplistic vision.

This is also true not only in the literary presentation but also in our human psychology. Individuals are not simply good or bad, to be pigeon-holed as specimens. They are bundles of contradictions, and the caricatures we make illustrate it. We have a tradition that poets and artists are libertines. They create beauty and yet in their personal lives seem to destroy order on which their artistry depends. We attribute cynicism to wealthy philanthropists but that is an easy way out. We think of politicians and used car salesmen as crooks, but that is not the whole story. We classify people by single adjectives, and we cannot explain how they then act in such contradictory ways to our adjectives. The better psychologists are aware that they are dealing with a creature too complex to be completely understood. We are unpredictable and free because of the raging conflicts for good and evil within ourselves.

Even philosophy is aware of this. The human being, we say, is a rational animal but the two words do not fit comfortably. In practice we seem to need to develop some dualism such as flesh and spirit and call one good and the other evil. Theologians keep encountering the problem of the natural and the supernatural. According to the theory both exist, and yet one always tends to gobble up the other. So when we apply these principles to doctrinal matters such as the incarnation or the "mystical body" or divine omnipotence and human freedom, we are often in trouble. The philosophical aspect is as much bedeviled by the contrasts as is psychology or literature.

The final note goes back to stressing that such conflicts exist in the decision-maker and are often not observed until brought into contact with the biblical text even indirectly. In moral decisions we do not have a problem until we have a conflict. We can all solve easily a number of theoretical problems as to whether we should beat and abuse children, lie to our own advantage, be sexually promiscuous, etc. As long as they do not touch us, we really have no problem.

The New Testament frequently uses the Old Testament to point up the real conflicts. Matthew 21:33–46 tells the very decisive moral tale of murder being plotted by the chief priests and Pharisees. It ends with Jesus citing Psalm 118:32: "The stone that the builders rejected has become the cornerstone." Then Matthew adds editorially: "They knew that he was speaking about them" (Mt 21:45). They did not even realize what the true moral problem was until he confronted them with a biblical text.

The great stories of the world's myths seem to recognize this. The hero who saves or who brings some great benefit to us is a hero who suffers. Whether it is Christ or Buddha or Mohammed, whether it is Odysseus or Marduk or some more obscure ancient figure, the story always involves suffering by the hero. The moral acts of the hero are not performed in some exaltation of nobility and efficiency. He must engage in a conflict which seems irrational and be brought to victory in some way which seems disconnected. The story keeps repeating itself in our human experience as recorded in literature. As mentioned before, Joseph Campbell has called him *The Hero with a Thousand Faces*.[7]

5

Faith

Graham Greene's novel called *Brighton Rock* has a marvelous punch line. A little English girl at the resort of Brighton falls desperately in love with a gangster. He despises her, but because he fears that she knows about a murder he committed, he marries her. She is, of course, a Catholic; getting married outside the church and having illicit sex suddenly seems to her the most marvelous thing in life. But then he wants to have done with her completely and persuades her that their love is impossible; only a suicide pact can keep them together. "You go first." But just as she is about to comply, the police arrive and arrest him.

She is walking past a church with this tragic love affair in her heart and impulsively goes in and slips into a confessional. She tells the "wheezy, old priest" that she is not here to confess her sins, but to tell him how wrong the church has been and that she does not want to live. The old fellow lets her ramble on until she runs out of breath and then half-listening says, "Well, just say three Hail Marys and I will give you absolution." She shrieks at him: "I don't want absolution; I want to go to hell." And he folds his arms and says, "Well, it's not that easy."

Greene's story is a marvelous example of the conflict between superficial faith and the real thing. We take it for granted that we believe in such things as mortal sin and hell and that we know just what they mean. There is a technical language for such things. Every word means one thing and every sentence has one literal sense. Our own society favors that and our usual scientific approach to the Bible does also. Historical criticism largely depends on defining the one precise meaning which the biblical texts had.

More recent study seems to have shifted attention from the goal of discovering the one decisive literal sense to considering the multiplicity, if not always an infinite range, of meanings in the text. Stories particularly lend themselves to multiple interpretations. Whether there are criteria of literature which limit the multiplicity of meanings is much debated. As has been noted, perhaps for the Bible the tradition of canon does limit the number of meanings in a sacred text. In practice most texts do not have simply one meaning for all readers, whether legitimately or not.

The problem is not new. Some thirty years ago Catholic exegetes in commenting on messianic prophecies tried to develop a theory called "the fuller sense" to explain how a prior writer such as Isaiah could have said something which did not seem very clear and yet which was applied to Christ in a perfectly definite manner by the New Testament authors. Such, for example, was the Isaian prophecy about a "virgin birth." It was theorized that the earlier text had a fuller meaning which was not totally understood by the original author but which it was the intention of the Holy Spirit to reveal.[1] The theory was intended to fit into the then prevailing scholastic idea of inspiration which asserted that the sense which was conveyed by the text (whether the original text or the reference to it in the New Testament) was the one which the Holy Spirit intended.

Since then we have begun to make some changes in our

underlying theory of inspiration.[2] Moreover, we have had to contend with newer methodologies which imply a different approach to understanding texts, such as structuralism, reader-response criticism, and rhetorical criticism in general. We now tend to understand that language cannot really be coerced into one simple mold at any point. Nor does the text cease to have life of its own in the readers as it passes from generation to generation. To understand, if not to justify, what the readers get out of it, we must have recourse to how the readers integrate texts into their own pre-existing codes of information and conviction and thus we may arrive at broader or different conclusions than the author intended.

For example, we may consider that virgin birth text of Isaiah 7:14. It reads in the New American Bible translation: "The virgin shall be with child, and bear a son, and shall name him Immanuel." Other translations put it somewhat differently but not by much.[3] Matthew 1:23–24 uses the text in these words: "All this took place to fulfill what the Lord had said through the prophet: 'Behold, the virgin shall be with child and bear a son, and they shall name him Emmanuel.' "[4] Luke doesn't cite the passage at all, but his story calls Mary "a virgin" (Lk 1:27). In his version, however, the child will be called "Son of the Most High" (Lk 1:32).

Before we ask how we should understand the prophecy, we should note how Matthew and Luke understood it. Neither quoted the text precisely. Matthew interpreted an indefinite Hebrew word for "maiden" as "virgin"; then he changed the naming from "she" to "they." Luke had the text in mind, but simply incorporated it into his story without citing it and changed the name of the child to "Son of the Most High." One further step should be noted. The post-apostolic tradition became much more precise and defined "maiden-virgin" precisely as a wondrous virgin-mother, both physically a virgin after birth and theologically the "mother" of God.[5] The matter was thus defined by the Catholic Church and this understanding of the text was canonized as having at least one clear meaning. Clearly the whole context of the then Catholic society's codes of belief was involved in this interpretation. However we interpret the text today, we shall also incorporate our encoded beliefs.

This is an example of doctrinal belief, but it does have its ethical overtones. Much of the dignity which Christianity brought to women in the centuries after Christ was based on the image of the mother of God. Sometimes the physical virginity was made into a rather rigid code of morals for women, ignoring the fact that the basic approach in the authentic tradition was the marvelous effect of God's grace upon a woman. As in the ancient myths of virgin goddesses, she was the human figure who bridged the gap between human beings and the divine persons. That does affect our moral stance but in a much more generic way.

We have come to reexamine many of our other interpretations from a similar change in stance. At one time parables were considered exemplar stories. We should be generous to the poor lest we end up like the rich man who neglected poor Lazarus (Lk 16:19–31). We should stop to help strangers in trouble like the good Samaritan (Lk 10:25–37). We should receive the word of God like the good soil, not like the rocky ground or that which was full of briars and thistles (Mk 4:1–9). And so it went. It was often a straightforward process of identifying specific images and stories with their presumed counterparts in our lives.

Then we began to observe that many of these stories were not very realistic. No one ever encountered an ending such as the rich man and Lazarus, since the story ended after death. The mustard seed that grew into a great tree never existed. Farmers are not so foolish as to scatter seed on roads or in thorn patches. No agriculturalist ever developed a machine which could harvest the weeds on the first sweep and the good grain on the second. On closer inspection the parables usually gave exaggerated pictures, and the outcome was paradoxical. The net gathers all kinds of fish, good and bad. But what was the net? The net was the Christian community. It should not be that way. But the parable says that this is what the church would actually be, and one had to live with it.

Madeleine Boucher popularized the name "the mysterious parable" for this phenomenon.[6] The crux of the parable is this unexpected turn of events and the problem of identifying our real life situation with what the parable is picturing. So also in the stories of discipleship we do not have a self-evident attempt to sell people on becoming disciples. The gospel writers depict Jesus as stating his demands bluntly and without limit; his promised rewards are vague and futuristic. "If anyone wishes to come after me, he must deny himself and take up his cross daily and follow me" (Lk 9:23; cf. also Mt 10:38; 16:24; Mk 8:34; 10:21; Lk 14:27). "Whoever loves father or mother more than me is not worthy of me" (Mt 10:37; cf. Lk 14:26). It is not the kind of reasonable selling job which we would try.

John's picture of Jesus is particularly strong on faith as the central point in discipleship. His specific commands are such as: "Love one another as I love you" (Jn 15:12), "Eat my flesh" (Jn 6:53), "Keep my commandments" (Jn 14:15), etc. They are never based on rational principles, but simply on appeals to what I say and what I do. The appeal and challenge was always to believe in this person and in the reality of an unseen world in which he moved.

Some theologians approach ethics on the basis of the call to discipleship.[7] The New Testament evidence is strong that the call and the following of Jesus was what shaped the way which Christians followed. Central to all the gospel stories is the decisive moment when Jesus revealed that his mission would be accomplished through his suffering and death (Mt 16:21; 17:12; Mk 8:31; 9:12; Lk 9:22; 17:25; 24:26 and in Jn 12:32 by implication). The call to follow him in suffering is always rejected to some extent (cf. Mt 10:38; 16:24; Mk 8:34; 10:21; Lk 9:23; 14:27 and John in the passages cited above). It is a pragmatic teaching which Paul believes is essential even when he runs into opposition over it (cf. 1 Cor 1:17–18; Gal 5:11; 6:14). All the subsequent decisions of Christians to suffer persecution, to be different, to trust in the Lord and to help others were based on this fundamental acceptance of suffering while doing good.

THE SUFFERING HERO

As Joseph Campbell has pointed out, in mythology the great hero must always suffer.[8] One does not work salvation by suffering, however. The sadistic approach to morals which says that if it hurts, it must be good, makes the great mistake of establishing causality. Not many people make decisions on that basis. The converse is more often true in our experience; we shy away from the honest decision because it spells trouble. That, too, makes the mistake of cause and effect. What the myth-maker perceives is simply the experience that salvation comes together with suffering. Consequently, difficult decisions become more acceptable.

In our biblical literature this point is made by paradox, irony and questions. The immense irony in Jesus' question to his disciples in the discourse on the bread of life (Jn 6:67, "Do you also want to leave?") is that he has not made a reasonable case for accepting his teaching. As he himself remarked, "No one can come to me unless it is granted him by my Father" (Jn 6:65). "Does this shock you?" (Jn 6:61). The text has involved us, as the words involved them, in a decision which we alone can make. But now we know that there is more to it than a simple command which we can fulfill externally.

Such also is the "messianic secret" which for years has been highlighted in Mark's gospel. It is not, as sometimes presented popularly, a ploy to conceal the identity of Jesus as messiah for political reasons. The secret is that the messiah is also the Son of God. The enormity of that statement still has not clearly dawned on us. Fourth century Christianity defined it with enough practical clarity as meaning that Jesus was both a human being and the divine being of God and yet one. That clarifies the texts although it escalates the riddle. Many of the stories in Mark need to be interpreted in the light of that canonized meaning.

Mark may seem to confuse his whole story at the end (Mk 16:1–8) by leaving the women at the tomb "trembling and bewildered."[9] However, in the light of Mark's literary technique the meaning clearly is that Christians should boldly proclaim that Jesus is the Son of God despite all the counterindications. The meaning of "Son of God" at the beginning of the gospel (Mk 1:1) may need explanation, but the explanation must be governed by the traditional interpretation of the whole gospel and even of the additional canonical material which was added in Mark 16:9–20.

Another example of how the meaning of texts comes to be opened to deeper meaning can be seen in John. How John can attempt to recast the already existing stories and interpretation of Jesus as the suffering servant foretold by Isaiah and still make his gospel come out as a Book of Glory is a teasing hypothesis even on the purely literary level. The first six chapters picture him as a misunderstood and rejected teacher. The last chapters, especially the passion account, picture him as a majestic, superhuman character who is identified with the Father and who dominates all the actions, even those that result in his death. What the reader may get out of this breathtaking paradox seems unlimited. The gospel is simply the literary opening into a life commitment. The later tradition, however, defined many of these specifics from the true nature of the bread he would give as related to his oneness with and yet submission to the Father.

It is not only story, however, which partakes of this mysteriousness. Poetry, especially prophetic poetry, abounds in contrasting images. As noted before, no biblical prophet is ever presented as a prophet of consolation alone nor as a prophet of doom alone. True prophets are both at the same time and without compromise on either end. In one of the most dramatic scenes in Jeremiah, that prophet is freed from the yoke around his neck by "the prophet Hananiah" when he accepted the government's propaganda that the yoke of the king of Babylon would be removed within two years (Jer 28:1–11). But Jeremiah had second thoughts, and he quoted the proverbial saying that "from of old, the prophets who were before you and me prophesied war, woe and pestilence" (Jer 28:8). It is the false prophets who are reasonable and balanced. Jeremiah reversed himself and prophesied that a worse yoke would be placed on the people. Then he reversed himself again and prophesied that a day was coming when the Lord would make a new covenant with the house of Israel and bring them back (Jer 30:3 and 31:31–34).

Proverbial wisdom, although apparently a middle-of-the-road approach to life, is nevertheless basically a paradoxical contrasting of one segment of experience against another. None of the other major literary divisions in the Bible is as strongly "moralistic" as wisdom; by its nature it is geared to instructing the young on how to live. The consensus opinion among scholars today seems to be that wisdom depends on a strong creation theology which sees the world as good. Psalm 33:5, which is in this tradition, has a common expression of it:

The earth is full of the goodness of the Lord.

Qoheleth can pursue his tongue-in-cheek criticism of mankind because he believes in this so strongly.

> One man out of a thousand I have come upon,
>   but a woman among them all I have not found.
> Behold, only this have I found out:
>   God made mankind straight
>   but men have had recourse to many calculations (Eccl
>   7:28–29).

It is cynical and blasphemous unless one is such a committed optimist that one can believe in spite of the evidence to the contrary. In the wise man's moralizing there is neither philosophizing nor argument; there is simply acceptance of experience as reflecting order which a good God put there. It may be that Qoheleth relied on more faith than we would think proper, but it is a faith approach.

METACOMMUNICATION

The church-goer who listens to a sermon and applies everything said to someone else is simply being dishonest and refusing to face the hard task of examining personal problems. The problem is within the hearer. I remember a student in a homiletics class giving a sermon on Paul's great chapter on charity in 1 Corinthians 13. The student sermon had the obvious conclusion: If we all loved one another, there would be no problems. I asked the equally obvious question: What if there is someone in the audience who cannot, at least now, love anyone? That happens. Applying 1 Corinthians as a commandment to love simply increases guilt. It is also a distortion of the

text by the preacher who has not thought through the gratu-
itousness of the gift of love.

Stories are harder to escape. As noted before, we tend to
identify with characters in a story. If we interpret all biblical
stories as hero tales, it is very easy to identify ourselves as the
heroes. However, we have seen evidence that the Bible does
not usually move in this direction. If we are honest, we try to
grasp the overall direction of the story and reinterpret it in the
light of our own background of information, conviction, criteria of rightness or wrongness, goodness or badness. This is
going beyond what the author really wrote, but it is inevitable
and the best fruit of our personal creativity. It is communication beyond what the words themselves say; it is metacommunication. This is what reader-response criticism is all
about.[10]

Comedy is especially valuable for discerning the hidden
meaning and the faith behind communication. Qoheleth tells
the amusing parable:

> On the other hand I saw this wise deed under the sun,
> which I thought sublime. Against a small city with few
> men in it advanced a mighty king, who surrounded it and
> threw up great siege-works about it. But in the city lived a
> man who, though poor, was wise and he delivered it
> through his wisdom. Yet no one remembered this poor
> man (Eccl 9:13–15).

Now within the framework of this story we are led to
assume that the poor man was the hero. We laugh because of
the irony in his being forgotten. Yet the author implicitly
invites us to step outside the terms of success and failure
which we have assumed within the story framework to contem-
plate another set of realities. The text tells us that the poor
man was truly wise. We laugh because we have been trapped

by a conventional system of values which we unwittingly accepted. This is called metacommunication. The perception has pragmatic value in psychotherapy. Paul Watzlawick of the Mental Research Institute of Palo Alto notes:

> Human relations in general are an area in which paradox can arise easily and inadvertently in the course of trying to overcome difficulties. Since we feel real to the extent that a significant other confirms or ratifies our self-image, and since this ratification will serve its purpose only when it is spontaneous, only an ideal case of human relatedness could be free from paradox. [11]

Again Watzlawick remarks:

> . . . many of the noblest pursuits and achievements of the human mind are intimately linked with man's ability to experience paradox. Fantasy, play, humor, love, symbolism, religious experience in the widest sense (from ritual to mysticism) and above all creativity, in both the arts and the sciences, appear to be essentially paradoxical. [12]

Shortly after Watzlawick quotes William F. Fry:

> During the unfolding of humor, one is suddenly confronted by an explicit-implicit reversal when the punch line is delivered. The reversal helps distinguish humor from play, dreams, etc. Sudden reversals such as characterize the punch line moment in humor are disruptive and foreign to play, etc. . . . But the reversal also has the unique effect of forcing upon the humor participants an internal redefining of reality. Inescapably, the punch line combines communication and metacommunication. One receives the explicit communication of the punch line.

> Also, on a higher level of abstraction, the punch line carries an implicit metacommunication about itself and about reality as exemplified by the joke. . . . In this reversal of content, what seems to be reality can be presented in terms of what seems to be unreality.[13]

The process occurs spontaneously in the hearer/reader or not at all. Hence, our traditional injunction: never try to explain a joke. Yet when one does laugh, one should understand why one laughs.

I offer a humble example of "metacommunication" from an old vaudeville joke.

A. "Had bad luck driving over here."
B. "Yeah? What happened?"
A. "Cut my tire to pieces."
B. "How did that happen?"
A. "Ran over a milk bottle."
B. "Didn't you see it?"
A. "Naw! Kid had it under his coat."

Now there is nothing funny here as long as one stays within the "real world"; it is simply a tragedy that a child has been killed. Of course, if one is a cynic about the value of human life, it simply gets worse. Laughter comes when we realize that we have been led down a path of normal values and then find ourselves facing in the opposite direction. This is the true function of comedy—to transport us to a different world of reality, and usually one that depends on faith, not on the logic within the story.

So in the Johannine story of the temple cleansing, the punch line is: "Destroy this temple and in three days I will raise it up," and the editorial comment: "But he was speaking about the temple of his body" (Jn 2:19–21). A word study of "temple," "body" or "raise it," such as historical criticism would use, will yield only peripheral results, and a study of the "form" from a form critical basis will not yield much more. One must step outside the story. The narrator has already given the readers privileged information in the Prologue where he identified his main character with the immortal creator-God. The readers already know by faith that this man cannot be destroyed. The people in the temple did not know this. Their misunderstanding is ironic; they miss the metacommunication which is the function of the story.

It is within this context that I speak of comedy in the Bible and for my purpose I group under comedy such techniques as irony, misunderstanding, paradox, antithesis, etc. They are different in form, but have a common function in communication.

Occasionally in our experience one catches a glimpse of an audience reaction which is so bizarre that one knows immediately that it is wrong. I remember seeing the movie "Tora, Tora, Tora" in Hawaii just down the road from Pearl Harbor. In the scenes in which the Japanese strafed the barracks and slaughtered indiscriminately, the audience cheered. They seemed to be reacting out of a love of violence rather than out of patriotism or sympathy which was the underlying supposition. They identified with the Japanese pilots as heroes rather than with the American victims. The metacommunication was misinterpreted.

A difference in audience reaction, however, may be perfectly valid. "Feminist theology" is often narrative based. The interpretations women put on stories, particularly about women in the Bible, are often distinctively different from those of their male peers. From an experimental psychology basis, women moralists such as Carol Gilligan have noted that women tend to interpret stories—including their own—on the basis of relationships and caring, not on who is right and who is in charge, as males do.[14] This leads to a different moral perspective. From a literary viewpoint stories are open to such divergent interpretation because that is the nature of story. They appeal to us differently because of our specific individuality. As Aristotle said, the reader is the most important element in the triad of author-text-reader.

Much of historical criticism has been devoted to revealing the underlying particularity of the culture and historical circumstances in which various texts were developed, written and edited. This has been called the *Sitz im Leben*, the life situation. It is certainly valid. However, to get from "there" to "here" we must recognize our own life situation as the matrix in which we will interpret the text. Unfortunately, not a great deal of attention has been paid to many of these problems. Women ethicists have begun the task and some men have begun to follow them.[15]

THE LAW

We need first of all to clarify our ideas about biblical mandates. That question arises in any Christian system of ethics. If from a biblical viewpoint the Mosaic law is considered a direct divine mandate, or, if it is the natural law divinely approved, then we conclude that it is timeless and unconditional in application. Practically speaking, we are not prepared to accept this since we must then include all the specific social and cultic regulations, many of which are not to our liking. Some biblical texts and some contemporary fundamentalist attitudes seem to presume that biblical mandates are all divinely revealed, although fundamentalists can be equally choosy.

First of all, from a viewpoint of biblical scholarship there is inconsistency within the Bible about the obligatory force of sayings called "law," "testimonies," "judgment," "statute," "word," "commandment," etc., especially in the Old Testament. The specific binding force of these various words which concern everything from worshiping one God alone to not boiling a kid in the milk of its mother is often problematic and never really discussed in the Bible. There is no one overarching definition for all such injunctions. "Natural law" as the guiding principle behind biblical laws is quite foreign to both Old Testament and New Testament thinking; if we import it into the text to help us clarify meanings, it should be recognized as an import.

Even our use of the word "code" to refer to biblical laws is non-biblical verbally and conceptually. In the Old Testament most of the laws seem to come from customary Semitic law, perhaps tribal. What is distinctive seems to be the apodictic ("You shall not . . .") laws of the decalogue which are not usually found in non-Israelite law. The other "codes" usually attribute the laws directly to God. The Hebrew law does so also, but it is distinctive in positing a covenant based on fidelity and love as the matrix. Although Israelite laws may most often have been similar in content to pagan law, the whole concept of law was different. Israel saw laws as "divine words" which communicated knowledge of God. So there is the frequent command to "be holy as the Lord your God is holy." One learned about God by living in a holy way.

The New Testament simply uses *nomos* for law in general and *entole* for specific laws. This terminology is not frequent in the gospels, although Jesus in Matthew 5:19 clearly says that he has not come to abolish "the law" but to fulfill it. The meaning of "fulfill" is quite unclear from this one usage; Matthew is noted for his "fulfillment formulae" and they are never a literal fulfillment of some text of the Old Testament. What also hinders a clear understanding is a clouded meaning of "law" in Paul. In Paul *nomos* seems more often to refer to the legal texts of the Torah, although not exclusively. Paul's judgment upon it is ambivalent; sometimes it is judged to be good and holy, but the law also "produces wrath" (Rom 4:15; 5:20; 7:9; 2 Cor 3:6; Gal 3:19). However, most important is Paul's perception that the Torah or law derived its force from the covenant with Israel and that covenant has been abolished (or fulfilled, as Matthew would say). Now that Christ has taken the curse of the law upon himself, no one is subject to it (Gal 3:13). The law is not bad in itself, but it is transitory. It was a tutor which took the child to school, but when the child grew up, it no longer needed the tutor (Gal 4:1–4).

More indefinite than "law" is parenesis or instruction. It is found mainly in the wisdom literature of the Bible. That literature which runs through Proverbs to some of the letters of the New Testament was intended to be mainly formative of the character of the chosen people. It was not legislation. Mostly it is a meditation on what is behind folk wisdom concerning successful ways of living. As such it is more understandable from the rhetorician's viewpoint than from the legal viewpoint or from an historical critic's method.

Instruction aims more at persuading to action than convincing through logic. The deeper aim is to penetrate behind the scenes of observed reality to see the hidden action of God the creator at work. This is especially true of New Testament wisdom. Two examples must suffice for illustrating the point.

The Sermon on the Mount—Matthew 5. The sermon on the mount, especially in Matthew 5, is becoming more recognized as a wisdom text. It begins with a traditional set of blessings ("Blessed is the man who . . .") which is right out of Psalms and Proverbs. The point of the discourse is announced in Matthew 5:17: "Do not think that I have come to abolish the law and the prophets. I have come, not to abolish them, but to fulfill them." Chapter 5 concludes with the punch line in verse 48: "In a word, you must be perfect as your heavenly Father is perfect."

This is an *inclusio* as the rhetoricians say: the beginning in verse 17 and the ending in verse 48 both use the same idea of completion, just as we set off paragraphs by indentations.[16]

The five examples used to connect the introduction to the conclusion are concrete and antithetical ("But I say to you . . ."). These antitheses are held together not by a logical development, but by persuasion which arises out of the images which are disparate, and yet pleasing. The original Old Testament texts behind verse 48 (Lev 11:44; 19:2, etc.) are themselves a definition of the God behind the "laws" and give an insight into why one should want to act in this way. This then defines the identity of the chosen people. In effect, they define believers as people who imitate God.

Haustafeln or "lists of household duties" appear in Ephesians 5:21–6:9, Colossians 3:18–4:1, and 1 Peter 2:13–3:7. It is notable that the biblical lists are restricted to duties within the household; hence, *haustafeln*. They do not concern public order. The order in which they appear—husband/wife, parents/children, master/slave—seems fairly consistent in all sources. Such pairs of exhortations are also found in Stoic writings, but are not distinctively Stoic. They are also found in rabbinic writings of a later date and in Iranian sources preceding New Testament times.[17] They represent customary wisdom on maintaining order. They are aimed at preserving familial society; none of them are aimed at a radical reform of society.

The literary form is made up of twos, and normally seems to imply a contrast on the superior/subject line of command. Although the introduction of the English word "submissive" into our translations seems to presume that wives are subject to husbands, children to parents, etc., the biblical texts really mandate nothing of such a hierarchial order. We are all equal in submissiveness to God just as Jesus was (1 Cor 15:28). This is the point of these texts.[18] What is notable about the biblical texts is the motivation which they give for these customary relationships. Even scholars seem to agree that the distinctiveness of the Pauline texts lies in the christological orientation. The emphasis is not on the "duties" as such, but on the "in Christ" or similar expressions which form the insight for performing duties which would normally be done anyway. Markus Barth remarks at the end of a lengthy treatise: "The content of the *Haustafel* is thoroughly permeated by references to the Lord. Step by step it is totally dependent upon the reality and validity of Christ's work and his presence. For this reason it is impossible to reconstruct from it supposedly 'original' Jewish or Greek tables of moral advice, and to assume that their 'Christianization' took place by adding a series of glosses. No pagan ideology or social pattern can be Christianized by sugarcoating. The ethics of Ephesians is in the so-called *Haustafeln* as much as in its other main parts an original witness of faith, and an invitation for a genuine public testimony to Jesus Christ who created 'one new man' (Eph 2:15) out of a divided people."[19]

The distinction which Karl Rahner and Josef Fuchs make concerning transcendental and categorical acts is very central here. Perhaps the terms are too abstract to have much meaning on first sighting. Let us substitute: what's behind the law and what is up-front. Behind the law (using law in the broadest sense) is a person whom we are seeking. In the Christian's case that is God or Jesus and eventually ourselves. What is up-front are the various mandates. Those arrangements for living in society have always come from the experience of the people. They are more or less wise, more or less practical, more or less actually observed. They always have some authority behind them ranging from jail sentences to disapproving looks from society. Often some more abstract authority is adduced, such as the state or God. Whether at their best or their worst, such laws, regulations, customs, normal ways of doing things, etc., deserve to be looked at before we make decisions.

This is the "tutor" stage in our decision-making. Paul considered the Old Testament as binding in prior time because of a covenant. So Paul introduced the idea of children and tutors in Galatians 4:1–7. Now, however, the covenant has been dissolved, and we are free. In this new age Paul roots the Christian's moral decisions on a "renewal of your mind, so that you may judge what is God's will, what is good, pleasing and perfect" (Rom 12:2).[20] The "tutor" stage is being left behind.

However, Paul himself makes some absolute demands, and those not only in basic morals. This, too, is "tutor." Paul asserts that his Corinthian converts are still in the "infant" stage (1 Cor 3:1–4). Paul is realistic enough to understand that perfect Christian maturity is not a given; it is probably not true for many and possibly not true for any across the board. We are all still "infants" in some ways and need the tutor. Hence the concept of *ecclesia mater et magistra*, the church as mother and teacher, still comes into play. So also does the morality based on natural law. The understanding of natural law has been around too long for us to ignore it in our decision-making.

HOW DO WE KNOW?

Philosophically, Catholic teaching has most often followed the Aristotelian-Thomistic theory of knowledge. We apprehend things and identify them; then we make a judgment as to which go together. Even in this philosophy we use the imaged expression "the light of natural reason" to explain how it happens since we don't really know. In Catholic theology we then admit a "supernatural light" of revelation which enables us to affirm things not knowable by human reason. We also bring in a supernatural power to accomplish good actions, and we call that grace. On these preliminaries our understanding of inspiration has depended for many centuries, and on them we have usually interpreted biblical morality.

This theological explanation, sometimes a caricature of what the theologians were really saying, has always encountered difficulty, and we are trying to improve it.[21] At times it became very mechanical and virtually destroyed free will or creative activity in the biblical authors. The final theological system may be so logical as to be inhuman and may ignore almost entirely the paradoxes which exist in the original beliefs, the "deposit of faith," as it is called. The basic doctrines of Christianity all appear to us as paradoxes. Jesus Christ is truly man and truly God; the eucharist really looks like bread and wine but is truly the body and blood of Christ; God knows everything before it happens and wills it into existence, but we are free to do what we will, etc. In accepting the deposit of faith theology cannot later explain away the discrepancies or compromise them. Yet it must erect a logical explanation of how they go together. This has affected our theories or ethics and our practice of morals.

Christian decision-making combines in its total process the rational element of logic and the faith element of accepting the underlying paradoxes. This is the way the Bible presents our story by calling us the images of God. It is also the way in which Jesus Christ is presented. The story is as full of mystery as the nature of the agents is full of mystery. The conflict between good and evil is not rationalized, but dramatized; the forces involved are too large for human measuring. Yet it is this very element of mystery which makes the definition of human beings realistic. At the moment when we make a faith decision to trust that God will help us to be something more than a "rational animal," we discover new potentials within ourselves.

We are now back at the beginning. The first statement in

this chapter was that the conflict eventually concentrates on a necessity for a conscious act of faith. Seen simply as literature, the basic story forms (hero, tragedy, comedy) all involve an act of faith. In the hero stories the faith is in oneself as the hero who can surmount the difficulties which the story-teller throws up.[22] In tragedy we have the story of faith betrayed. In classic Greek tragedy Iphigenia is destroyed by the gods who do not listen to her prayers. In the story of Jephtah in Judges 11 the innocent daughter is betrayed by her father who values his oath above his daughter and so sacrifices her. Saul is destroyed at Endor by an implacable Samuel who represents the God who does not repent—an unexpected turn of events. Especially in comedy we have faith in some outcome which is not logical or predictable, but fitting. "Christ has died, Christ is risen, the joke is on the devil." The other forms of literature in the Bible follow a somewhat similar pattern.

This is indeed the way in which we are confronted within ourselves by the moral decisions we make. There are few apodictic answers to some of the most commonplace occurrences. Shall one spank the child or hug it? At best, one trusts that what one does will turn out well. Should one turn the other cheek or challenge the aggressor? Christ advised the one (Mt 5:39) and did the other (Jn 18:21–22). Should one cast out the sinner from the community or forgive endlessly? Matthew 18:15–35 advises both. The list can be expanded indefinitely from biblical examples. Such conflicting images cannot be harmonized by textual manipulation or clever interpretation or logical harmonization. It is part of the literary context that the paradox exists in the text because it does so in the reality of our lives. We define "moral agent" in practical terms by such literature.

It was noted previously that rhetoric began as the art of effective presentation and persuasion. Logic eventually went its separate way; persuasion became the province of rhetoric. Artistic literary presentation often involved an insight into contradictions that logic could not cope with. At its worst, it became sheer sophistry and gave rhetoric its bad name. But at the best it recognized a higher integration than logic was able to offer. The court jester was both a fool and a wise man. The orator appealed to something more than logic—and so we remember those marvelous speeches which Shakespeare minted for Macbeth and Brutus and Hamlet, etc. The conflicting claims of life and death, fame and shame, glory and defeat were not compromised, but became acceptable as enshrined in a person and we knew that we had experienced them ourselves. It was not simply a matter of playing with the emotions, but of integrating "what the heart knows" with what common sense demanded. The paradox and irony noted above are not simply clever literary devices; they are part of our instinctive decision-making process. They appeal because we are like that. At this point the literary art turns into psychological reality or the reality of who we are which is the ontological level.

Faced with this dynamic of conflict within ourselves we turn to faith in something or someone. We cannot prove that our decision is right. We may say "conscience" or "feeling" or "instinct," but these are simply names for a faith, however incipient, which is within us. What the crisis makes us do is to examine the reality of our faith, and hence of ourselves, more deeply. We arrive at a better understanding even if we do not know for sure how to solve the problem on our own. Experience teaches that often the problem is solved for us if we have the patience to persevere.

Much of Mark's gospel is built on this dynamic. In Mark 3:22–30 Jesus is attacked by the scribes who make the strange accusation: "By the prince of demons he drives out demons." Jesus uses the example of the household torn by strife to refute that nonsensical rumor. But he does accuse them of a more mysterious blasphemy against the Holy Spirit. None of this seems to be very clear to us today. Nor does it seem to have convinced the scribes to change their way of acting. However, the story form employs what is called Mark's "envelope technique" (Mk 3:20–21 and 31–35). Another story surrounds this one. At the beginning his family has heard of his preaching and "they set out to seize him, for they said, 'He is out of his mind.' " After the confrontation with the scribes, the family arrives and is announced to Jesus. As he gazes around him at those seated in the circle, he continues, "Whoever does the will of God is my brother and sister and mother." These people are the opposite side of the scribes. There is little logic in the whole story; there is much of faith accepted and faith rejected. And then they continue to be seated around him.

6

The Person

2001: A Space Odyssey, the first great space movie, ended with the only surviving astronaut, Frank Bowman, finding new life as a baby. He had tracked down the mysterious force behind TMA-2, the monolith discovered first on the moon. Alone in a sterile but luxurious suite he aged into an old man and in the final scene was reborn in the womb. Curiously Arthur C. Clarke wrote the novel after the movie was made. In the written story he was able to bring out more clearly what the visual presentation intended. Frank Bowman was not afraid; indeed, he felt that he was finally coming home; his life on planet earth had been an alien existence; he belonged here. Whatever the force behind TMA-2 might be, it or he/she was benevolent and welcoming. However, Frank Bowman never got to know who the person behind it all was.[1]

"No one has ever seen God" (Jn 1:18). It is a truism, but that has never prevented us from trying. Samuel Terrien in *The Elusive Presence* has made a study of how stories in the Bible try to capture a picture of God and how he always escapes.[2] As the title indicates, Terrien has tried to tie together all the major themes of the Old Testament and New Testament by the concept of the presence/absence of God. Eventually, the thesis does not succeed (as do none of the others),[3] but it is certainly a noteworthily good try.[4]

Among the stories which Terrien interprets is the final episode of Moses on the mountain demanding to see the face of God (Ex 33). God does not refuse; he recognizes this as a good and necessary human drive, as the story of the garden of Eden recognized that the original pair would want to be like God. The story begins with Moses rather peevishly complaining to God about being put at the head of an ungovernable people and then being given no support. Moses finally tells God bluntly that he is tired of being saddled with this burden and that if God wants this people to be his people he will need to come along with them. Even that does not satisfy Moses. He personally wants to see the face of God. God tells him that this is impossible, but that he will compromise. He hides Moses in the hollow of a rock and then puts his hand over Moses as he passes by in his glory. When God takes his hand away, Moses gets just a glimpse of God's backside as he passes by. It is a marvelous artistic tale of what we have been seeking since the garden of Eden. Moses the great law-giver is not seeking some more laws; he is looking for the person of God.

All great literature has this personal note. In our own writing a good math textbook is much appreciated, but the name of the author seldom becomes a household attraction. We can admire the beauty of the bridge which we are crossing, but we do not instantly ask about the name of the engineer. We know a few names in medicine of doctors who have discovered major remedies or procedures, but when we go to a doctor, we are not greatly interested in the name of the discoverer of the medicine. However, when we go to a play or a concert or choose a book, we want to know the name of the author or performer. In the arts the first thing which is revealed is the artist.

It is the nature of the literary enterprise to reveal the nature of the author or narrator, and in this respect literature seems to mirror life. It also reveals who we are. When we read the morning paper at breakfast and comment on the news, we do not simply report what the paper has to say. We "hrrumph" and laugh; we smile and approve; we frown and condemn. In short, we reveal far more of ourselves than we reveal of what is in the paper.

The dedicated listener picks up the same from casual conversation. The non-consequential details of daily life fly by us in words, and only occasionally do we find one that merits stockpiling in our memory for possible future use. What we do assess and store away is our impression of the speaker. He is loud, boastful or conversely quiet and thoughtful; she is full of gossip and innuendo or kindly and prudent. We note which ones make themselves the heroes of all their stories, which ones make themselves the tragic figures of life, and (God bless them!) which ones can laugh at life and themselves.

The biblical stories are often great literature. Someone is revealed.[5] The biblical authors generally take the stance of an anonymous, omniscient narrator. We can detect only a little of the historical Isaiah or Matthew or "author of Hebrews," often too little even to define them as "individual authors." They do not reveal much of themselves. Conversely, they most often reveal much in a few words spoken by their characters. The gospel of John is noteworthy for this technique.

John 4 is the story of the Samaritan woman. It is a story in the wisdom tradition. The discourse concerns weighty matters about worship and faith, not about some specific moral case—unless one wants to say that he was preaching about divorce, which is certainly not the point. More specifically, it is a story about the identity of people. The story abounds in remarks such as, "If you knew . . . who is saying to you, 'Give me a drink . . .' "; "You have had five husbands, and the one you have now is not your husband . . ."; "I know that the Messiah is coming . . ."; "I am he . . ."; and the later, "Come see a man who told me everything I have done . . ." and "We have heard for ourselves, and we know that this is . . ." The point cannot be missed; by the end of the story the character of all the actors has been revealed. Most of all the character of Jesus has been revealed, and as the omniscient narrator said in the Prologue, "The only Son, God, who is at the Father's side, has revealed him" (Jn 1:18). God had been revealed.

This is the way in which the unseen God becomes known in the Bible. Paul's phrase "in Christ" has for many centuries been recognized as central to his theological insight and his moral applications.[6] The moral applications are not there for the sake of law-making, but for the sake of revelation. Take Paul's attitude toward slavery. Paul never said that slavery was good. He saw slavery as a fact, and he used the Old Testament image of Israel as God's slave to encourage slaves to see their condition in that light. "Be slaves of the Lord Christ" (Col 3:23). The distinctive notion here is the identification of the Christian with Christ.

Neither did Paul mandate inferior roles for wives and children in the family. What he did do was to give a new insight into customary realities now that people had been converted to Christianity. Here also the key was his expression "in the Lord" (Col 3:20; Eph 6:1). So also what Paul was examining in the "household duties" was not a series of moral cases defining the rights and obligations of husbands and wives, masters and slaves, but a perception of something beyond the accepted custom which revealed a new insight now that people had been converted to Christianity. It is somehow by being personally united to Christ the Lord, by accepting his same "submissive" attitude (Col 3:18; Eph 5:22), that we become truly "Christian."

We may have quite different conclusions than Paul on the

specifics of all these relationships today, but we are challenged by Paul to give our own deep insight into the presence of God/Christ in such existing or proposed customs. Mere flouting of "rights" or expected psychological outcomes does not make us competitors of Paul. The specific decision to social problems which we or the church may propose may be reformable or only one of several alternative right or good ways of acting; the need for finding the presence of God/Christ in the situation is an absolute. "Where's God?" is the supreme test of ethics.

THE IMAGE OF GOD

Since no one has ever seen God, we must go about defining this person by what we see within ourselves. "The image of God" is a dominating metaphor from the beginning of the Bible (Gen 1:26—"Let us make man in our image and likeness") to its final maturing in the New Testament.[7] The context of Genesis 1:26 is that "God saw that it was very good." That context is consistent in all the rest of the Bible. Luke 15:11–32 tells the story which we have (mis)named "The Prodigal Son." The prodigal son is only peripherally relevant. The father in the story is clearly the central character and a stand-in for God. What the father says is not "You are forgiven" but "You are my son." That is the point which he makes so clearly to both sons that the final meaning cannot be lost. To the reader as well as to the characters in the story, the appeal is not to imitate somebody, but to recognize who one is, and to know that the son is like the father.

Catholic moral teaching in the past few centuries unfortunately centered more and more on cases of what was mortal sin and what was venial sin. Inadvertently that created a picture of God as judge, mostly a hanging judge. It functioned the same as hell-fire and damnation does in some other sects.

What was obscured was the older Thomistic emphasis on virtue as morality. The garden of Eden story became a sad tale of original sin (a term which the Bible never uses) instead of the mysterious quest for the tree of knowledge and the tree of life. The real problem with morality was not guidance for doing right deeds, but the lack of recognition that the Christian does not simply do righteous deeds; the Christian becomes Christian by trying to be like God. The Christian is constituted Christian by them, is "divinized," or, in the older terminology, Christ is both exemplary and efficient cause. In a way we are our own creators. Mortal sin is truly mortal; it kills the image of God. Acting as a Christian expresses the divinity within us.

THE CANON IN THE COMMUNITY

The search for identity is not simply a matter which the individual pursues in isolation. We are not like Frank Bowman landing alone on a remote planet. We have a sacred scripture which we all hold in common and which holds us together. Recently the study of canon and inspiration has taken a new start among scholars after having been neglected (or deliberately avoided) for a good number of years. We are now studying inspiration, which is an associated part of the problem, not as an isolated act of God communicating with one person, but as a process involving the whole community as it was shaped by events, interpreted as God-directed, formative of their lives and eventually recognized as "sacred" writings.

All of the actions within this process aid the identification of a group. The Bible, both Old Testament and New Testament, defined the chosen people. You could tell who they were by the kind of God they accepted, the kind of worship they gave to that God and the kind of demands which they understood that God was making upon them. "I am your God; you are my people" was the Old Testament formulation. "The church," "the body of Christ," "the true vine and the branches," etc., were among the many metaphors used in the New Testament to express the same idea.[8] Such always defined a community, not an individual.

Jews were recognized among their neighbors by how they worshiped and how they lived; so too were Christians. The principal charge eventually brought against Christians by the Roman government was that of atheism, i.e. they worshiped not the state-approved gods, but a certain "Chrestos." They were clearly different in a way that people could see. They were also set apart by the way they lived: "See these Christians, how they love one another!" was an ancient slogan we remember even to this day. The morals came from a basis in faith, and the morals defined them more vividly than the more abstract theology.

So the record of the sayings and deeds which they remembered became the "canon" or measuring rod. In this sense canon was not just the decreed list of books—that happened centuries later—but the process by which the people defined who they were. The books were important because the community accepted them as foundational, as Karl Rahner has pointed out.[9] One was a Christian if one accepted these books; one was a heretic if one either abridged or expanded them. The abridging was especially distasteful to the fathers.

A concomitant problem arises with the canonization of the books of the Bible. It is central to Christian belief that a certain set of books should be canonized as the rule of faith and of living. The books were canonized only slowly through the first four centuries. They were canonized first by popular acceptance in circumstances which had moral and doctrinal overtones. It is noteworthy that the major decisions about the nature of Christ were made at about the same time that the books of the Bible were canonized with some final authority circa 400 A.D. It is notable also that the final de fide decision on the canon was only made much later at the Council of Trent in 1542—and it was the first decision the council made—and that decision was followed by many doctrinal and some moral decisions which were tied to specific texts and to specific contemporary problems.

Does canonization not simply imply a decision about which books belong in the Bible but also carry with it some implication of interpretation of specific beliefs and ways of acting? If so, how does one track down these implications, especially in ethical problems? The study of canon is really just beginning to reveal a new understanding. At any rate, the study is beyond my competence but it should be remembered.

Canonization is being studied with renewed interest today not simply as a series of historical dates at which certain books were accepted by some authority, but rather as a process of development by which people expressed their own identity. They said in effect: "These books tell what we are all about!" This leads also to a new interpretative methodology called "canonical criticism."[10] The final text which they accepted became in some way authoritative interpretation for the holders of that tradition. The primary source of interpretative authority must be found among those readers. Those readers or hearers have continued to reinterpret the message throughout history. In Christian tradition that reinterpretation, often multivalent, can be found with varying degrees of authority in the writings of the popes, the councils, the fathers and the later theologians, lay or clerical, men or women.

More specifically the source of this confidence in text and interpretation was understood as coming from the Holy Spirit. The Spirit, of course, was frequently associated with the giving of the word both in the Old Testament and in the New. The operative term to describe these books was "sacred." "Inspiration" was a common and non-distinctive attribute in early Christianity; many of the fathers called their own writings and those of orthodox Christians "inspired."[11] A similar phenomenon occurred in rabbinic Judaism. In later Christian ages "inspiration" became a term restricted solely to the "inspired text," and "grace" became the operating factor in teaching and preaching. This acute separation of terms was needed, but perhaps has misled us.

The Holy Spirit continues to act upon the readers as once that divine influence impelled the authors to write. The bugaboo of inerrancy, even inerrancy of every conceivable kind, has become something of an irrelevancy in contemporary study except in the more generic sense mentioned by Vatican Council II: "Therefore, since everything asserted by the inspired authors or sacred writers must be held to be asserted by the Holy Spirit, it follows that the books of scripture must be acknowledged as teaching firmly, faithfully, and without error that truth which God wanted put into the sacred writings for the sake of our salvation."[12] The specification "that truth which God wanted put into the sacred writings for the sake of our salvation" considerably limits the extent and quality of inerrant teaching.

COMMUNITY INTERPRETATION

Josef Fuchs, the Catholic ethicist, has drawn a line between rightness and goodness.[13] An action is not Christian because it is right, but because it is good. "Right" means that which conforms to right reason; "good" means that which embodies moral goodness. An action may be mistakenly considered as "right" even though it is "objectively" wrong—the traditional case of the erroneous conscience. It may nevertheless be good. On the other hand, rewarding an employee with a higher position in the hope of having him stumble over the greater responsibility is never good. It may be the right administrative thing to do, but it is not Christian.

The only real test of rightness in the Christian community is the decision of the community. It is the community, the people of God, which in the long run is the guardian of the tradition.[14] Professional moralists must give opinions, but no matter how solid their reasoning nor how great the consensus among them, there is no final "objective" answer. The consensus may go a long way to persuade us; the officials of the church may use moral pressure, but the church is not a policeman. Even if the church were to make an infallible pronouncement about a moral problem—which it apparently has never done—we would not have an "objective" but an infallible decision. The line of goodness does not rely finally on reason, but on faith.

The computer analogy may serve several purposes here. The software has codes embedded within it which tell the computer how to operate. In a word-processing program, a few of those codes may be easily accessible; even the novice operator can safely change them. A modestly competent programmer can get into the program itself and change some of the other hidden codes. However, the programmer may exceed the limits of competency and inadvertently disturb other parts of the program without being aware of it. In fact a "virus" may be created which will eat up the data or even the program. A skilled programmer may change all of the codes, but with difficulty. The computer works logically, but it may escape our slippery grasp on logic.

Tradition is something like this. We have been "trained" as Catholics; we have codes embedded in our social reactions. We respond almost spontaneously to some moral problems. Some of that training comes from an authentic understanding of the faith. All of us, as is true of the faithful down through the centuries, have held to the basics of the doctrinal statements as irrevocable. That is tradition, the de fide part of our belief. Those are the most deeply hidden codes in the computer program, except that in this case they are completely protected. But then through the centuries we have also acquired many lesser convictions or "traditions." They are like the unprotected codes, but they have varying degrees of difficulty if we consider changing them.

Somewhere in the past few centuries we made an effort to classify the firmness of such teachings by "theological notes"— e.g., de fide, proximate to faith, theological conclusion, common opinion and even a humble note bringing up the rear guard which was called "offensive to pious ears." This never quite worked. As with the computer program, once we began tinkering with the hidden codes, we were never quite sure how it would affect the whole program. In a curious way this affected moral decisions, and here there were no de fide conclusions.

For example, we once thought that usury was wrong, pure and simple. As our modern industrial and banking world developed, we were forced to change our opinion. Slavery was once accepted as normal and at least suffered to continue. Now we consider it unacceptable. Sexual morality has certainly changed and that largely at the roots, although we do not clearly understand what we are doing to the whole system of symbols, social organizations and education.

Biblical sexual attitudes were healthy and joyous. Sexual sin was certainly known, but it was not so much sin of the body as sin of relationships. Sexual intercourse was expressed as "knowing" someone; the sin was in the improper knowing. But these Semitic attitudes shifted when the early fathers began to change the hidden codes to Greek concepts of body and soul instead of the old biblical way of talking of "self."

The Latin Vulgate of the fourth century A.D. already manifests some of this change. For example, Paul's advice about abstaining from intercourse for the sake of prayer and then returning to the normal course of relationships ends with this observation in Latin: "I say this by way of indulgence (*secundum indulgentiam*)." The Latin means approximately what the similar sounding English does. The original Greek from a Semitic author clearly said: "by way of suggestion" (*kata suggnomen*). The later Latin translation, reinforcing the Greek dualism of body and soul, seems to hint that one needs some sort of permission or forgiveness for "indulging" in sex.[15] The attitude, once introduced into the tradition, seemed to spread through the program although the church never condemned sex outright as evil or less perfect. It came close to it in the practical consequences.

On the other hand, many virtues were instilled into the attitude of Christians by the tradition. Human dignity, humility, patient endurance, self-sacrifice, etc. were never formally canonized by the church either, but were borne along for centuries by Christian ways of living. They were borne along mostly by specific examples of the saints.

Which of these ingrained attitudes were authentically biblical and which were not is the entangling question. As has been made capital of in this book, the biblical attitudes themselves were often presented as paradoxes so that both attitudes could be beneficial.

In Catholic theology the continuing reinterpretation comes under the heading of magisterium ("teaching authority") with all its multiple distinctions and certitudes or persuasions. In general, revelation can be defined from this standpoint as "the written record and faith-recollection of particular entrances of the divine into the realm of the human as recorded by Jewish and Christian faith communities which experienced them and continue to live by them. Thus, Christian biblical revelation is that written history and recollected experience, not only as it has been recorded in the Bible, but also as it is now being appropriated (continuing revelation) in the human and religious experience, knowledge and understanding of those living in a Christian faith community; i.e. in people attempting to live according to the reality and consequences of these divine entrances into the realm of the human."[16]

The union with others in the church is perhaps the most important and distinctive part of Catholic ethics. "Neither the author nor the community works in isolation. What the biblical author wrote arose from the community and was destined for the community. So also the reader must be aware of the community as a source of interpretation and as recipient of communication from the reader. Such community influence on the decision-maker extends beyond one's immediate community to the historical and Catholic community which must have a voice in witnessing to and interpreting the action of the Holy Spirit."[17]

Protestant biblical ethicists often express this, although less vigorously, as the formative action of the community upon its members.[18] This is where the bulk of such ethical influence started, namely with the wisdom tradition which was more formative than normative among the clan (to invoke Gerstenberger)[19] and later among the people of God. It has surely been operative throughout Christian history especially in our catechetical endeavors.

The Catholic position goes farther in insisting that the influence is not only formative, but can also be normative. So in the traditional phrase we call the church *mater et magistra* (mother and teacher). That church is not simply the local community or the sect, but the "catholic" church throughout the world and throughout history.

To cite a brief example, the Bible does not deal with such modern questions as the pill for use in birth control. The effect of the encyclical *Humanae Vitae* was not to define infallibly a doctrine, but to act as mother and teacher in interpreting the mystery of begetting human life. Numerous biblical texts can be cited for the generic teaching that human life must be respected. Basically, we are to imitate God who is the life-giver. The specifics are an attempt to understand the meaning of this within a contemporary human situation, a situation in which we need to live out our identity as church and Christian. Within the individual who must make the decisions, this interpretation must be given weighty consideration. However, it is not simply a matter of adding up the logical reasons on both sides; it is also a matter of admitting that the Holy Spirit has an influence on the decision which is finally made. Seeing God in the decision-making which may roam the whole field from a desire to provide the best for the child to the cost of a new set of maternity clothes may be the most difficult part.

THE LEAP AND CHALLENGE OF FAITH

Theology has always struggled with the basic premise that it must accept its givens from a non-logical source. The whole emphasis of theology as a science is on logical arrangement and connections. Consequently, it has a mind-set of avoiding whatever cannot be logically discussed. Scientific ethics of any sort has always contended with this as well; when it becomes Christian ethics, it seems to contradict its own nature.

When the Bible is used with the intention of adding something to rational ethics, it is the historical methodology of biblical study which presently has the most appeal. However, historical criticism like rational theology is not very good at contending with matters of faith. It can investigate whether a certain group of people actually believed a certain doctrine at a given time, but that is about as far as it can go. In itself it has no real appreciation for faith since that cannot be investigated for historical logic. It also has no real appreciation of literary artistry which is a more sensitive interpreter of faith. In practice, however, biblical critics often ignore both of these limitations and present their own conclusions about theology and the beauty of literature, but they do so without warrant from their own science. This has been the common status of biblical morality for many centuries.

Obviously historical criticism, along with all other legitimate forms of biblical criticism, has great value. All of these represent experience, both the experience which facts assure us existed in the past and facts concerning the historical critic's own present situation. The broader such a study of facts is, the more helpful it is for us to understand contemporary problems. Scholars presumably are familiar with many such facts, especially of the past, although they sometimes seem singularly limited in their experience of the present.

In tribal societies or among families with a strong sense of tradition, the uneducated may often have a greater living awareness of how the past matters and be open to understanding and expressing how they are part of that stream of story. When they are confronted with decision-making, they may be able to bring a Christian heritage to bear on the problem without much conscious reflection. We are not talking simply about custom here, although that may, indeed, be a factor. We say that such people "think as Christians" and that explains it all. So also there are many people of common sense and clear-eyed faith who are better at making decisions than those who have highly sophisticated educations and confused values.

Such people may not be able to give a very convincing explanation for their actions. The story is told of Francis of Assisi that he opened the book of the gospels and allowed the first verse he encountered to determine his future: "Sell all you have and give to the poor. . . . Then come and follow me" (Lk 18:22). The process may be indefensible on rational grounds. In other similar stories, it may be indefensible on any grounds. In the case of Francis it was the right decision. The determining factor in either case is not logic. Nor is Christian decision-making a process of rationalization before the fact which can then be demonstrated to have led to the fact. This may be all right in a murder trial in which the prosecuting attorney demonstrates that the accused planned and cold-bloodedly executed the crime. We do not really act that way very often.

THE PERSON

This book has tried to use the Bible to illustrate how decision-making takes place. Previously a distinction was made between the levels of literature, psychology and ontology. Psychology has not helped us much since we do not have much experimental evidence as to how the decision-making process takes place. On the philosophical or ontological level we have had many theories of "human acts," but the necessary distinctions between the intellect and the will, between the acquiring of knowledge and the applying of it, have tended to distort the wholistic understanding of the total process which involves our emotions and physical well-being. Literature remains the most accessible foundation of reflection on the whole process. Obviously, also, a treatise written by a scripture professor must proceed from what he knows best.

Stories are illustrations of how the whole human being works. An alcoholic who tells his story will not have a lot of theories, but he will have many dramatic incidents, good and bad, to relate. He is a bundle of conflicting images and emotions. The final conversion comes when he makes the unprovable decision to turn his life over to the care of God and he probably has a new image of who God is. That is what makes story-telling succeed—the honest portrayal of the conflict and struggle to survive amidst all these forces. That is the total human being, neither entirely noble nor entirely bad. It is at that gut level that the real decisions of life are made—by everyone, not just by scholars. Indeed, in world history scholars have not been notably the most important decision-makers; only Plato in *The Republic* believed that.

The Christian decision-making process is both communal and personal, but always a decision of faith. We all make decisions without often adverting to how we are doing it. "The decision-making process lies in the at least implicit perception of the operation of faith at all stages in the decision-making process from composition to individual decision in act."[20] Faith does not simply add motivation to decisions by a Christian. Supernatural virtue does not merely build on natural virtue. From the biblical evidence it appears that faith is both the beginning and the end of decisions concerning discipleship. "Come, follow me" is not the conclusion of a syllogism, but the initiating invitation which makes it possible.

In almost all of the reasonable theories we have studied of how the Bible relates to ethics and morals we have discovered that the best approaches all end in favor of a wholistic approach to the Bible. Using the biblical text as exemplar, using it as normative in specific mandates, tying it all together with an overarching thematic point such as love or grace or freedom, etc.—all these have a limited legitimacy and usefulness. In the final analysis the most ancient tradition asserts itself: the Bible is the word of God. It is not simply words; it is a unified whole, however disparate it may appear in places. From the prophetic saying: "Hear the word of the Lord, O Israel" to the Johannine comment on Christ: "And the Word became flesh" we have a consistent understanding that God's communication with us is not a mumbling of disconnected phrases, but a communication of himself, the one, the unique. The limitation to understanding is within ourselves since we do not apprehend all truths in that simple fashion. The whole history of the human race is from his viewpoint a single act glorifying himself.

When we try to apply this to human acts which are necessarily discreet and very limited, we run into difficulty. "Be holy as the Lord, your God is holy" or "Be perfect as your heavenly Father is perfect" is indeed the essential mandate (Lev 11:44; Mt 5:48). But we do not really know how the Father is perfect; we read of some of his actions which give us a clue, but not all. That can be confusing. The author of Sirach noted centuries ago:

> For who can see him and describe him?
>   Or who can praise him as he is?
> Beyond these, many things lie hid;
>   only a few of his works have we seen.
> It is the Lord who has made all things,
>   and to those who fear him he gives wisdom (Sir 43:33–35).

We must use our limited knowledge as best we can, and we are assured by Christ that he is with us. The church can discern those things which are necessary for our salvation. But salvation takes place amidst the drama of human struggle, and we do not often know with certitude as a faith community what the specific demands are.

The crucial question in this community search for goodness is: What is the authentic tradition? In our society polls have become the measure of how much consensus exists. We have become experts at the sampling process with its plus or minus such and such a percentage. Obviously, this is not a report on the decision of the community, much less a measure of the Catholic faith which has always and everywhere been held to be the truth. That sixty-five percent of American Catholics do not presently accept the teaching of *Humanae Vitae,* or such and such a percentage do not agree with the U.S. bishops' statement on the economy, or that the majority do not believe that priestly ordination should be a permanent commitment, etc., does not represent the real *sensus fidelium*, the belief of the apostolic and catholic church. The pollsters themselves know how varied are the people they are labeling as Catholics and that they have little information as to how representative they are. We all know this intellectually, but polls are things we can see and image; as we have noted from the beginning, images have a great influence on our decisions.

Most of our public dialogue is conducted largely on the basis of image-making, whether we are talking about war and peace, racial equality, life at its beginning and its end, relations among nations, candidates for office, etc. All the major topics get presented to us on TV, in newspapers and magazines, and by orators who are still rhetoricians. The images gang up on us. They are not invalid, but they do not yield truth simply by being winnowed through the sieve of logic, much less of the latest poll.

The real dialogue which clarifies the rule of faith is a long process. It, too, is expressed in images. One of the most curious heresies in the history of the church was over the cult of images or statues. Presumably many of the iconoclasts and their opponents never understood the theological underpinnings of the argument. People could see the statues and pictures of the saints which were standing in churches or which they wanted banned from them. Many moral decisions were made during the crisis. A lot of churches were burned and a great number of people persecuted over images. That they could understand. The final verdict was in favor of the images.

PERSONAL DECISION-MAKING

What is distinctive about Catholic ethics is the clear role of the community tradition in the process. However, many of our most important decisions eventually come down to a lonely moment of truth. It may be that the community cannot be present to us in the personal way which we need. Such, for example, may be the trauma of dying. We may have signed a living will and indicated our intellectual convictions. However, acceptance of the impending reality of death may be a different thing. Shall we accept the Father's will or shall we fight for life against him? The final decision must be a personal one.

Then there are situations in which the individual Christian finds a personal dissonance with the community consensus. Those in authority may be acting within legitimate bounds and yet the subject may feel reason in conscience for disagreeing.[21] Academic freedom or rights of appeal may be involved. The dissenter stands alone.

In both such circumstances more is involved than simply making the right decision in one particular case. The basic Pauline approach to ethics is the initial statement to Romans 12–15: "I urge you therefore, brothers, by the mercies of God, to offer your bodies as a living sacrifice, holy and pleasing to God, your spiritual worship. Do not conform yourselves to this age but be transformed by the renewal of your mind, that you may discern what is the will of God, what is good and pleasing and perfect" (Rom 12:1–2). The first sentence here is crucial.

By "offering your bodies" Paul refers to the whole person although the emphasis is on external actions. Such is his usual way of using "body." Everything we do is to be seen as a "living sacrifice." However, the everything we do is not to be viewed as a check-chart of right actions. The mature Christian knows from within what is good and pleasing and perfect. "The renewal of your mind" in Paul's terminology is not a philosophical concept but an understanding of life which comes from the experience of conversion. That is what allows us to discern the will of God.

So what Paul is saying is that we discover ourselves, we become Christians, when we act on what we know has happened to us. We become children of God. We do not solve all our problems. In honesty we know that we are still incomplete and contain contradictions. But God as we know him is like that too. The Bible presents us with a whole art gallery of pictures of God. They do not go together neatly. God is lover and judge, ruler and confidant, remote and within us, silent and Word, etc. Only a person, as we know from our human experience, can gather together such divergences. We seek a person and we ourselves become like that person.

True enough, the church is always there as the teacher. But the final decision as in any classroom belongs to the students and it proceeds from their goodness—or lack of it.

Honesty is the prime requisite. The many images in which problems of decision-making come to the individual need to be sorted out. Prejudice, human passion, previous codes of conduct from family, society, peers, all crowd in upon the Christian and distort judgment. Some of these existing impulses are truly Christian, some secular, and some sheer evil. To face oneself honestly, to sift through all these codes which trigger action and finally to construct a new image which meets this precise situation, is a daunting work of art and faith. Prayer, obviously, is a most necessary factor in surviving as a Christian. It not only illuminates; it attracts to us the power of God. "No one can come to me unless the Father who sent me draw him, and I will raise him on the last day" is the saying of Jesus (Jn 6:44).

The synoptic gospels all tell of a preaching mission of the disciples commissioned by Jesus. Matthew 17:14–21 has a report on what happened. Although they followed his instructions, they could not cast out a devil from a possessed boy. "The disciples approached Jesus in private and said, 'Why could we not drive it out?' He said to them, 'Because of your little faith' " (Mt 17:19–20). They had made the right decision, but they did not have the goodness to really believe. Matthew always attributes at least a little faith to the disciples. Mark is more inclined to say that they did not understand. But the next remark is curious in Matthew and may not even belong to his text: "This kind does not leave but by prayer and fasting" (Mt 17:21). It may be a floating saying, but at least, it represents an understanding in Matthew's community. The images involved in the decision-making process were not complete until the power of prayer and fasting had been introduced to show how the complete decision functioned.

7

How Do They Say It?

What is man that you are mindful of him?
or the son of man that you should care for him? (Ps 8:5).

So began the ancient meditation. Some shepherd poet standing under the stars in the desert looked up to the heavens and asked the central question of the universe and its maker. On the answer to that question will depend all the practical decisions which we make. Otherwise, who cares?

We now need to review some of the bases for the method which we have been using in investigating ethics. As we have already noted, the philosophers of Greece whom we have followed for centuries began with an abstract answer to "Who am I?": man is a rational animal. The choices which we make are good or bad depending on how well they help us fulfill our total potential as a rational animal. From that beginning the scientific scholar develops other basic premises, logical arguments and specific conclusions which finally say: this action is right, this action is wrong. Deviations can be admitted into the system only on the basis of an escape clause for conscience; one must always do what one's conscience dictates whether it is objectively the right decision or not.

The desert psalmist started with a different answer:

You have made him little less than the gods,
 you have crowned him with glory and honor (Ps 8:6).

In his world good and bad were not judged by objective norms
of the deeds themselves, but by the stature of the person he
was. For him that person was a kind of god and closely related
to the one God called Yahweh. He was expected to live up to
the glory and honor which had been conferred on him. He had
to dig out of his own experience and the traditions of his
people just what that meant. Essentially, his decision was a
judgment on the person, not on the action. In this approach
"good" and "bad" are much more a relationship between two
persons (especially God and the human being) than a relationship of an action to a principle. This was an ethics built far
more on moral agents than on moral actions.

Our previous chapters have proposed defining "moral
agent" from stories, not from statistics or from philosophies.
That is what people normally do. People tell of their problems
as stories, not as bare-bone, factual cases which can be num-
bered and filed away. The stories never have a final ending as
long as we are alive to tell them.[1] Yet we are persuaded by these
stories. Rhetoric rather than logic is the principal ingredient
both of our thinking about ourselves and in the way we talk
about our experiences. It is also the Bible's way. The difference
is between an "action-centered ethics" and an "agent-centered
ethics." This needs to be examined in more detail.

HOW WE TALK ABOUT WHAT WE ARE DOING

Even the language we use is different in the two approaches. The difference between "cases" and "stories" provides an opening point. We use technical language to describe
one and common language to explain the other. Technical lan-

guage in any field is intended to be "objective"—i.e. it states what is known of facts in terms which can be universally understood in the same sense by all. "Measles" means the same to doctors all over the world. Local languages may use a different word, but even that is not frequent. "Doppler effect" means the same to physicists everywhere. It says nothing about how the doctor or the physicist feels about the thing and even less about how the patient feels. Common language, however, abounds in feelings, images, contrasts. It reveals something of who we are as much as it reveals what we are thinking about. Literary language is akin to common language in that respect. It reveals feelings. On the other hand, it has something of technical language's precision. For a story or a poem the word must fit precisely, and it must feel right.[2]

Our quickest way into the world of the Bible is through stories, and they are increasingly used in theology.[3] Stories are like motion pictures. They are made up of individual images. Their impact depends largely on how well the artist captures the precise feeling and appropriateness of the scenes. They are "moving" in that emotional sense as well as in the sense that the story is going somewhere. It is going either to a satisfying climax of triumph or to a piteous defeat or toward a comic ending. These are the basic forms. The hero story (either epic or personal) links characters and events in a logical sequence which moves toward the victory. It may be a concealed sequence as in a good mystery novel or an obvious ending as in a national epic. The tragedy is even more irresistibly logical. It portrays a hero with a fatal flaw. Inevitably it is that flaw which destroys. Comedy is the most difficult type to bring off. It is not logical; the ending is a surprise. But it is fitting. That is why we laugh. We shall need to say more about the comic technique.

The Bible is astonishingly adept at story-telling. Saul, as we saw, is a fleshed-out character although a minimum of words are used. We know how he feels even without the explanation which I gave. It is also a self-contained episode within a larger story. Aristotle remarked that a tragedy is a story which begins absolutely and ends absolutely. There is no possibility of a story about the return of Saul. On the other hand David is a hero and so numerous stories must be told about David. We identify with the hero and want to be like him, not just once but over and over. So our television series continue until we are tired of them. Comedy confounds everything, logic as well as feelings. Comedy in this sense is the Bible's strong point. If God is God, then it is appropriate for him to act in ways which are beyond human logic and control.

The plots of stories are told largely through the characters. The best stories are those in which the characters are truly representative; then we can identify with them. Yet the representations must not be caricatures, pasteboard cutouts. They must be individual as well as representative. They must have not just logic, but emotion, deep and flouted. Shakespeare's Hamlet and Macbeth and Juliet are clearly defined individuals. Yet we all recognize a little of ourselves in these characters.[4]

Isaac Singer, the Nobel prize winner of Jewish tales, once explained his art of story-telling by going back to the creation. Said Singer: When God created us, he gave us intelligence— not a great amount, but enough to know how to survive. Then he gave us will power—not a great deal, but enough to keep our heads above the water. And then he gave us emotions— gallons and gallons of emotions. That is what story-telling is about. It is about the combat between people with boiling passions who have just enough intelligence and will power to control something, but not enough to dominate. That is also what decision-making is about.

Poetry follows somewhat similar lines. Poetry revels in images and contrasts, and that sometimes makes it seem odd.

"The prophet is a fool, the man of the spirit is mad," Hosea says (Hos 9:7). He sees things which other people don't and he puts them into such compellingly different words that we must listen. This is not to ignore that there are often symbols which are traditional. Indeed, the tradition of symbol is often what gives effect to the poem. It is recognized and savored because it is known and calls up a whole host of emotions. This is true of all good or traditional art.

"Oh, say can you see by the dawn's early light," immediately stirs up in us Americans pictures and emotions. It is not the logic of the words nor even their beauty which affects us, but their symbolic meaning. Bernard Lonergan noted that "literary language tends to float somewhere in between logic and symbol."[5] Just where nobody has been able to define. So the book of Lamentations is a heaped-up series of laments on the guilt and punishment of Judah that leaves no acceptable understanding of how a good God can do such things to his own people. Yet the images speak of a more hopeful past and in spite of harsh realities engender hope again. As Norman Gottwald remarked, "When history has become unendurable, faith endures."[6]

The instructional parts of the Bible are perhaps the most difficult to assess on literary criteria. By instructional I mean "the laws," "the commandments," "the precepts," "statutes," etc., especially in Deuteronomy, the sermons, proverbs, essays and letters. The Old Testament is sometimes referred to collectively as the law by the Jewish and Christian tradition. The sermon on the mount is sometimes called the new law. These instructional designations certainly do not all fit into one neat category, but they have something in common which leads me to group them here. They are all searching for something or someone behind the scenes.

At first reading these instructions seem to be directly in line with moral teachings which we are expected to follow. We are rather selective about observing them, but in general our tradition seems to assign them to some sort of legal status, religious or ethical. However, they never coalesce into what we call a code. There is no discernible central principle holding them together and they are not arranged in any kind of strict order. The New Testament does not even cite the whole of the ten commandments. Paul's instructions are all suited to a particular occasion and cannot, for example, be made into a permanent handbook of church order. Paul at the end leaves it to the community to do whatever seems proper.

Attempts have been made to identify the laws of Deuteronomy, or at least a great number of them, as the civil code of the Judean monarchy. But this breaks down. Presumably Judah had a civil code and possibly the Bible parallels it in places. But the Bible curiously lacks all those mechanisms of police, courts and jails which are needed to enforce the law. The wise men who wrote Proverbs and other such treatises knew much about a proper order in family and civil life, but were notoriously unconcerned about connecting it with law, even with the law or the covenant.

Conventional Catholic morality has always recognized this human factor. We admit that there may be extenuating circumstances in any moral case. But we cannot really measure such factors since they are personal, not objective. Hence, we must give them a peripheral role. In biblical storytelling the extenuating circumstances, so to speak, may be the point of the matter.

Logic is the flesh and bones of science. It is the doorway into our control over the universe around us. However, science stops short of the boundary of explaining human beings. Human freedom is too mysterious. Rhetoric has always had the advantage of being able to accommodate immense contrasts and paradoxes. Logic abhors them. Yet in some ways rhetoric can describe human life more fully and more accurately.

LITERATURE REVEALS PERSONS

All of this is curious and at least hints at something else behind all of this instruction. It certainly says something about persuading people to be good. But it is not concerned with logical reasons or with precise norms. It is rather an insight into what is behind the laws.

Law-givers are revealed by the laws they make. Dictators conceal their personal needs under the many laws which they enact. The bureaucrat reveals himself by the minutiae of his laws, the indifferent by a lack of any order. The wise legislator makes few laws, simple and flexible and realistic. The foolish legislator produces reams of new laws each year. Law is revelation. In the Old Testament the giving of the laws is associated with the wondrous deeds of God. God has revealed himself by the laws as well as by his marvelous deeds in nature. So also Paul stresses that the coming of Jesus and his teaching is a new revelation. It is the person who is revealed. Like any person the law-giver is revealed as many-sided, complex, full of contrasts as others see him. God is revealed in the Pentateuch mainly as the liberator, the faithful guide and guard of his people. He is revealed in the New Testament as the Father and in his Son, Jesus Christ. Yet these pictures are never monolithic and one-sided.

If law is revelation, then it is not a science, but an art of communication. The revealed law has as much of humanity in it as of divinity. It is understanding which is sought both by God and by us. The essential question is not what must I do, but where is God both in noble actions and in repentance.

We must take this into consideration in biblical ethics. It is also suggested by recent developments in biblical criticism. The historical criticism of the past hundred years is well known and was aimed at objectivity. But in the past ten years particularly a whole new look has been taken at biblical methods.

AGENT-CENTERED MORALITY AND
RHETORICAL CRITICISM

Instead of asking the question: What really happened? (which is what historical criticism has been all about), the question now is: How does this text attempt to put across a message in language? I have chosen to call this approach "rhetorical criticism" although the expression is not universally accepted; "literary criticism" is probably becoming the more common term.[7] However, "rhetorical criticism" has an honorable tradition behind it and, most importantly, preserves that important difference between logic and persuasion on which much depends.

In recent times various kinds of rhetorical criticism have been developed by biblical scholars. It is a fascinating study of what happens when we use words. Structuralists are convinced that a structure of meanings underlies all use of words, and this structure is independent of particular languages, times or social and personal conditions. In a way it is a return to the Greek conviction that words represent realities—things and relationships—which exist even before we use words. Pushed to its limit, structuralists would claim that there is one and only one meaning to words, if one can discover it. In actual practice structuralists seem to end up at the opposite extreme by making words mean almost everything or nothing.

Quite different is reader-response criticism. Here the emphasis is on how the reader responds to words, not on what the words mean in themselves. Those who use this approach sometimes claim that there is an indefinite number of equally valid interpretations to any set of words. In reality, however, this does not seem to work. If you scream "Fire!" in a crowded theater, you provoke a hearer response. If the interpretation is false, you may be subject to arrest, as one of our chief justices has noted. On the other hand, the word "Fire!" printed on the page here does not evoke much response at all.

> The moon was a ghostly galleon,
>   tossed upon cloudy seas.

The verse from Alfred Noyes' poem seems to evoke varied emotions among readers. Yet if one says that this is sheer doggerel, the tradition of English literature which has canonized it resists. So with biblical texts; there are legal restraints and traditions of the community which restrict meanings.

We also have canonical criticism which studies the form or interpretation in which the text was accepted as sacred. One must take into consideration the expected faith response of the readers. There is here, however, another complication. Are we talking about the readers who were contemporary with the original author or about those who are our contemporaries? Or someone in between?

The most frequent use of rhetorical criticism thus far has been in narrative criticism. Stories lend themselves most easily to diagnosis as a means of persuading readers, which is why we so often use stories when we want to make our point.

After Vatican Council II encouraged a greater use of scripture in moral study, the first tendency for Catholic moralists was to quote more biblical texts and to quote them according to the findings of historical criticism.[8] This did not yield dramatic results; the immense shift in Catholic moral research has come from other causes. But it did reveal the inadequacy of doing more of the same. What we need is a look at biblical morality not from the viewpoint of our scientific ethics, but from its own self-understanding as literature. Perhaps we shall find some more suitable common ground at a later time; for the present we must be content with accepting the Bible for what it is, insofar as we can know that.

SUMMARY

On a more formal level what we have been investigating has been the difference between scientific ethics and the biblical approach. As a science ethics must produce a system of principles and conclusions—that is the definition of any science. The principles of the science of ethics begin with a definition of who the human subject is. In our traditional western view this has usually been Aristotle's definition of man as a rational animal. There are other views. Orthodox communism defines man as a social and economic agent of the state. Hinduism probably defines man as a creature on the way to being absorbed in the all-being or the nothingness. That makes a difference in what you will consider good and bad.

From this basic premise the science goes on to elucidate more immediate principles, such as: We make our choices on the basis of what seems good to us. We cannot choose something which we think is evil. We may be wrong in our evaluation, but we think it is good. In a choice between two goods, the common good comes before the individual good. Etc. How far one goes in this is somewhat uncertain. But we start with such general truths.

Since man is a rational animal, we must then construct a bridge of logic to the specific conclusions that we are searching for. That provides us with a list of specific actions which are judged to be good or bad. Since the problems are always changing, we need to be constantly examining the basic principles and the chain of logic. Personal variants do not fall under the system. We know from experience that there are extenuating circumstances of passion, ignorance, prejudice, etc. These, however, cannot be measured by the system. Besides, there is that great escape valve that one must follow one's conscience, whether right or wrong. The system is geared simply to produce a judgment on the "objective" right or wrong of the action.

Biblical ethics is quite different. There is no "system" of ethics in the Bible—no "principles," logical argumentation or conclusions. Instead we have a record of experience. It is either a "word of God" which they experienced or practical common sense which came out of their observation of how life turned out. Consequently, even the language which is used is different from the scientific language of ethics. Instead of abstractions and precisely defined words, we have the literary language of stories, poetry, wisdom sayings and laws which were conceived of as revelations of who God was.

As noted at the beginning of this chapter, when the Hebrew asked "Who is man?" the answer did not come in a philosophical definition but in a poetic insight of the relationship of man to the maker. The originating insight in Genesis 1 that man and woman were made in the image of God then dictated that they should act like God as much as possible. Such a rule could not be applied legally nor logically. What was sought was not objective conclusions on the rightness or wrongness of specific actions, but insight into the potential which the relationship offered. The technique depended not on logic but on persuasion. This was the Hebrews' way of using rhetoric. The end of the inquiry centered on the judgment of whether the individual was becoming more or less like God in the actions which were done. It was an "agent-centered" ethic. This has guided our whole inquiry.

8

Eschatology and Apocalyptic

As in *2001: A Space Odyssey,* any story must have an end, and the end must explain the story. However, Frank Bowman, the astronaut in the story, did not die. So how did we know that this was the end of the story? In the movie the screen displayed "The End"; movie time was over. That is one obvious and somewhat crude meaning of the end. We would have a quite different meaning in mind if we asked: "What end did the director have in mind?" End then means purpose. The New Testament sometimes uses the word to refer to the end time or *eschaton* and sometimes to purpose. Unfortunately, the meaning about an "end time" seems to take the show.

This has relevance to Karl Rahner's distinction between "transcendental acts" and "categorical acts," obscure and theoretical as that may seem.[1] A story in the second half of the Acts of the Apostles may illustrate the matter. The first telling of Paul's conversion (Acts 9:1–30) has him confronting a mysterious light and a voice. Paul's response to the voice is: "Who are you, sir?" (Acts 9:5). The problem centers on a person. The full meaning of "I am Jesus, whom you are persecuting" (Acts 9:5) takes a long time to dawn on Paul. The beginning comes three days later when he is baptized and "things like scales fell from his eyes" (Acts 9:18). But even then he needs to be accepted by the community in Jerusalem and spend more time meditating on his experience before he begins his real mission. This is a transcendental act on Paul's part. It transcends our normal decision-making and it transcends the usual reasons we have for making decisions.

On the other hand, Ananias also has a vision (Acts 9:10). He must make a pragmatic decision about visiting the persecutor, Saul, and there are good reasons against it. He cites the reports on this man and then argues with the Lord. The Lord wins the argument in a normal way by cluing him in on what is going on behind the scenes. This fits neatly into the category of conflict-resolution which we know. It is a categorical act. It fits a category which we know from custom, common-sense ways of acting, etc.

The end of these stories about Saul and Ananias is quite different. Ananias does what he is supposed to do; the job is finished and he vanishes from the story. Saul becomes Paul, and eighteen chapters later after long descriptions of being shown "what he will have to suffer for my name," he ends up for two years in a house in Rome under arrest simply receiving all who came to him (Acts 28:30–31). What an odd way for such a lengthy story to end! It is reminiscent of King Jehoiachin sitting forever at the table of the king of Babylon eating his daily allowance (2 Kgs 25:29–30). That is the odd way in which the long history of the kingdoms of Israel and Judah ends. The stories of Paul and Jehoiachin don't really end as far as the story-teller is concerned. They keep pointing to something more. They transcend our idea of where a story should end.

The matter is further complicated in biblical thought by the frequent convergence of eschatology or "talk about the end" and apocalyptic or "revelation." Apocalyptic is an odd sort of literary style which is usually cast in a dream or vision scenario. The conflict is not haphazard; at heart is a realization that human strife is far more serious than a simple battle between humans or a compound of weakness and ill-will. It is not just pedestrian gang-warfare or domestic strife.

Many a conscientious physician has suffered a trauma in his early medical practice. He had become skilled enough and experienced enough to have confidence in himself. And then one day he does everything right for the patient—diagnosis, treatment, personal care. And the patient dies. Often enough the doctor's reaction has been one of anger. He should have won. He had cast himself in the role of the great conqueror of death and he had been bested. Worst of all, he did not know who the enemy was. But he was sure that it was a someone, not merely a physical disease. It was a personal force and he resented it. No one in this world has ever explained this malignancy and identified what or who it is. We do tend to express it in personal terms.

In biblical terms a battle rages between Satan and a heavenly host. In the book of Daniel and in the New Testament a heavenly/earthly character called a "Son of man" is involved. The title seems to be the one Jesus chose for himself. Good always wins in the apocalyptic stories, but to the foot-soldiers on earth the battle always appears most confusing and uncertain of outcome. The literature is usually associated with times of crisis. Like a good politician, the author insists that something, usually rather general, must be done now. This is carrying the transcendental elements of decision-making to an extreme.

When the time element prevails in eschatology, it is rather simple to escape from moral dilemmas. One simply says that the time of trial is very brief and soon there will be an equalizing of justice. So we have a prevailing theory that the early Christians expected the world to end within a relatively few years.[2] It did not end shortly; supposedly the early Christians had to change some of their ideas, particularly about morals, and work out a philosophical ethics to replace the "interim morality" which the original message is said to have enshrined. As time goes on without the temporal end, we need to make more adjusting. So we exalt the obviously necessary need for change in a changing world.

APOCALYPTIC NOW

The problem with this is that there is little real evidence that the early Christians did expect an "imminent parousia" or coming of the Lord, although that is the usual opinion. The focal point for the presumed change in attitude is usually marked somewhere around 70 A.D. when the Romans destroyed Jerusalem. The home of both Judaism and Christianity was eliminated and the shock, presumably, convinced them all that a new age was dawning. Such is the theory that is used to explain the divergent texts which sometimes seem to expect an imminent parousia and which sometimes seem to stretch out into an indefinite future.

However, the character of apocalyptic seems to say that this is a wrong way to look at "the end." Apocalyptic was a literature which had a limited history, mostly between 167 B.C. and 100 A.D. Oddly, it produced no new writings around 70 A.D. which would have been exactly the time one would have expected.[3] D.S. Russell has no explanation for this. He does have an opinion as to why it went into an eclipse after 100 A.D. both in Judaism and in Christianity—namely, it proved counter-productive in the new social crises. So also J.A.T. Robinson, the well-known author of *Honest to God*, has objected that the imminent parousia conclusion is simply taken for granted without proof.[4]

All of the apocalypses demand action now.[5] What is most peculiar is that the predicted times for the imminent end came and went and did not seem to bother the readers.[6] Apparently they understood the "now" in a different way than we do. The "now" of apocalyptic is much more an exhortation than a chronological time.

Strangely enough, we understand "now" in contemporary propaganda quite well. Politicians and activists are fond of predicting imminent disaster unless we do something about the scoundrels in office or the destruction of the environment, etc. We never take it all that seriously.

APOCALYPTIC AND GOOD AND EVIL

Eschatology and apocalyptic are recognized as crucial problems for all who would discuss biblical morality.[7] What did apocalyptic add to eschatology? Both believed that history was tending toward a definite end. Apocalyptic interpreted history, however, as symbolic of a more cosmic history than our earthly one. It was transcendental. It was tinged with the dualism of good and evil; it saw the cosmic history as a battle between total evil and total good and it created brilliant images of warfare, including a battle in the heavens, to illustrate its faith insight. It had a pessimistic view of the present age which it considered as mostly in the control of evil. A cataclysmic event (not an evolution) must occur to allow good to destroy evil and usher in the new day.[8] The final cataclysm was a manifest judgment upon good and evil in which evil was seen as cosmic, not as petty "nastinesses committed behind a bathroom door," to use Archibald McLeish's vivid phrase in *JB*.

Eschatology on the other hand is earth-bound. From the time that the phrase "the day of the Lord" appears in Amos (Am 5:18) in the eighth century B.C. and down through Isaiah, Joel, Ezekiel, Zephaniah, and various uses of "the day," the reference is always to an historical event. The glorious day of the messiah is also seen within earth-bound history. Israel had a mission to fulfill which was of this world—to bring blessings to all nations. The church had a similar mission, and the church was to endure for that purpose (Mt 16:18). This, too, was within an earthly time-frame. It is categorical. Yet the category applies more within a community setting than within a personal one. Eschatology is connected with the purpose of an earthly community. Good and evil are to be judged not simply on personal grounds but on how specific actions affected the mission of the church. The distinctiveness of Christian ethics is connected with this.

This has meaning for the way in which we make our moral judgments. The categorical acts can be judged on the basis of right or wrong, especially as they affect the community. The transcendental acts never have an ending. Only at the end will there be a book of Revelation. We need to wait to see what will be revealed as the end of the story. In Matthew 25:31–46 we have such a picture of a final judgment of individuals on the basis of their actions within the community. However, although the sheep are separated from the goats, we have no information about any individual. We do not know who will be the sheep or the goats.

THE FAITH COMPONENT

Such an insight into good and evil can be made only by a person of deep faith who perceives the invisible or spiritual world. For others the struggle looks entirely like workaday problems with successes and failures; ethics is simply a question of crisis management. For the poet or the apocalyptist the

normal daily occurrences are decisive acts which can end only
by the agent being consigned to heaven or to hell—which was
another idea that apocalyptic introduced. Evil attained a reality and sharpness which was otherwise not perceived. What
happened as the Christian era began was not that a timetable
failed to be fulfilled, but that people became lax in the sharpness of their insight and commitment. Rudolf Schnackenburg
in his final conclusion to *The Moral Teaching of the New Testament*
notes that the early teachers of the New Testament were conscious of being bound by what Jesus said. "Vigorously and
unflinchingly, they proclaim Jesus' message to their own age,
mitigating nothing of the Lord's commandments and demands. Never since that time has the voice of those who proclaim the Christian faith and preach Christian morals fallen
silent; but their words were not always equally profound in
faith or equally powerful. One reason for this was no doubt
that many of them no longer understood Jesus' message in its
eschatological urgency. But only when this is presupposed can
we comprehend the radical demands made in the gospel,
which have the holy will of God as their sole guiding principle
and which could only be made in the light of the gospel of
salvation, of the coming reign of God which, in Jesus, is already at hand."⁹

So in the gospels (especially Mark and John) and in Paul
the transcendental struggle is not with flesh and blood but
with world rulers of this power of darkness (Eph 6:12). Demons fight against Jesus; they must be expelled. It is not a
petty conspiracy on the part of Pharisees or Jews which works
the murder of Jesus; nor is his message one of political insurrection however cleverly done. His is insurrection against the evil
one, and the demons know it: "What have you to do with us,
Jesus of Nazareth? Have you come to destroy us? I know who
you are—the Holy One of God!" (Mk 1:24). So Jesus could

talk of radical discipleship: "He who would save his life will lose it (Mt 16:25; Mk 8:35; Lk 9:24; 17:33; Jn 12:25—the only proverb to appear in all four gospels). "What could one give in exchange for his life?" (Mk 8:37).

What should be noted about this act of faith is that it is not faith in a theory of eschatology, but faith in a person. In the gospels it always comes down to believing in Jesus, not in a teaching or a law. Such also is Paul's teaching: believe in the Lord Jesus. Logic runs into problems when confronted with unknowables. Rhetoric, which more closely reports on life as it is, knows that humans are bundles of contradictions and yet manage to hold the whole disparate lot together in their persons. Getting to know God is the crucial point of living so that we may know who we are and who he is. Jeremiah complained:

> The priests asked not,
>   "Where is the Lord?"
> Those who dealt with the law
>   knew me not:
> The shepherds rebelled against me (Jer 2:8).

We have talked about a decision-making process which demands faith during the whole process of the deciding. Truly so; only faith can highlight the radical good and evil which is involved; only faith can interpret the images for what they are; only faith can make a realistic assessment of the conflict. Only then does a Christian know what the real choices are. They are not choices to obey a law or not to obey it. That may be the "front"; the real choice is radical alliance with good and hatred of evil. It is in that choosing which is manifest only to a person of faith that one discovers what it means to be a Christian.

And it is in that moment that one discovers who the God is who conquers evil. He is not "a nice guy" who simply and painlessly dismisses sin. Paul's concept of redemption (Rom

3:23–26) has no significance within that kind of concept of a loving God. "All have sinned and are deprived of the glory of God. They are justified freely by his grace through the redemption in Christ Jesus, whom God set forth as an expiation, through faith, by his blood, to prove his righteousness because of the forgiveness of sins previously committed, through the forbearance of God—to prove his righteousness in the present time, that he might be righteous and justify the one who has faith in Jesus."

God loves with a voracious appetite. There is something substantial at stake. This is not simply "motivation" which Christian faith adds to ethical decision-making; it is part of the substance of the process, as Daly insists in his "hermeneutical circle."[10]

RETRIBUTION THEOLOGY

In and out of the biblical considerations of ethics a retribution theology seems to flow. Popular imagination often rejects a considerable portion of the Old Testament (as Marcion rejected all of it) because it seems to portray a cruel God who ruthlessly destroys, sometimes for petty reasons. There is also a tendency in our culture to scissor out passages of the New Testament which seem to emphasize that evil is punished and good rewarded. We would prefer to picture a loving God who disregards such peccadillos. This can certainly be a problem for an "ethic of caring."[11]

The biblical evidence for a retribution theology is strongest in the Old Testament, especially in the Deuteronomist's history, the great account which runs from 1 Samuel to 2 Kings. At times that history reads almost like a Greek tragedy. David is punished for his sins of overindulgence; he has no escape. The essays on the destruction of Israel and of Judah (2 Kgs 17) attribute that disaster to the sins of the ruling classes or the people. As the Lamentations of Jeremiah so poignantly bewail, there is no escaping the punishment and no self-justifying is possible. This history is inexorable.

The New Testament is presumed to have changed all of this. But has it? If we exult that Christ did not accept the judgment of his contemporaries that the tower of Siloam had fallen on the eighteen victims because they were greater sinners than all the other men in Jerusalem (Lk 13:4), nonetheless he did adopt the apocalyptic view in his picture of the judgment. The separation of the sheep and the goats in Matthew 24 is absolute and based on merit. Hebrews has fiery admonitions not to backslide; there can be no redemption for those who do. There is a sin against the Holy Spirit which cannot be forgiven. Paul counts that salvation does in some way depend upon works. "Be sure of this, that no immoral or impure or greedy person, that is, an idolater, has any inheritance in the kingdom of Christ and of God. Let no one deceive you with empty arguments, for because of these things the wrath of God is coming upon the disobedient. So do not be associated with them" (Eph 5:5–6).

Retribution is simply an observation of fact. Play with fire and you get burned. No amount of love will protect you. Society punishes those who break the law. Abolishing jails or fines has never seemed very practical to most people. Deterrence and the equity of justice have always appealed as necessary functions of authority in society. The laws (and the judges and the police and the jailers) have been shaped to protect those who are set upon unjustly (cf. Rom 13:1–4). Punishment follows in its natural course when order is disturbed. A retribution theology always waits in the wings because it seems inevitable. We only try to create a theology which explains the facts.

This treatise has mentioned previously the need to protect "the law" (natural or positive or customary) as a "tutor." Nell Noddings struggles with the law in dealing with children as a behavioral problem.[12] When the child will not accept the responsibility for caring, then some punishment or deterrence must be invoked to protect others. Certainly we must admit a validity to both a "natural law" as well as a ten commandments which exists outside ourselves and which involves penalties for abuse. But it points to something beyond simple restoration of equality among humans. That leads only to a human conflict over rights.

Apocalyptic sees world history not primarily as a story of victory or defeat for individual human beings. It sees all of this and more as the victory of God. In the final analysis God does not take pleasure in punishment; he takes pleasure in his own glory. The "end" is the last and most decisive of his "wonderful deeds." The last act of the drama is the revelation not of the sufferings of the damned in hell but of the entry of Christ on the white horse.

Finally, one must consider a personal end. If you have cancer, then consult your local doctor or actuarial tables. If it is a matter of what life is all about, that is different. If one believes in free will—and it is a belief—one must consider that remaining faithful to the end is a moral decision, indeed the most important one. Christian piety has always esteemed final perseverance as a most special gift of God. Yet if one looks at most of the long-term commitments which one has made—and made with full knowledge and conviction, such as marriage, priesthood, a profession, recovery from an addiction, dedication to the poor—and how few of us die while still professing the same beliefs, then we can begin to understand that what was involved in the decision was not simply logic and determination, but that mysterious and supernatural factor called grace. There is a mystery in why we made the decision in the first place and why we have persevered or abandoned our first love. So the book of Revelation warned Ephesus: "Yet I hold this against you; you have lost the love you had at first" (Rev 2:4). That was the moral problem which the New Testament addressed by using apocalyptic. That is the problem which we face. There is no final solution except unquestioning loyalty to a person.

9

Nurse Lucille Revisited

Let us now reconsider our nurse's story at the beginning. What decision did she arrive at? Superficially, it may appear almost insignificant. At the beginning of the story Lucille was a competent and apparently satisfied professional nurse. At the end she was still a nurse and presumably an even better one, since she was at peace. However, there were changes. She had come in touch with something honest about herself. She knew herself better and she was willing to accept some of it.

If we ask what line of logic an ethicist might find here, we would be disappointed. We might take the psychological approach and say that she was simply "processing" the experiences of a long-ago and sometimes suppressed existence. This is not the logic of an ethicist or even of a scientist, but it seems to explain something if one is willing to accept that human beings are simply the sum total of all their experiences, and that is the end.

The ethicist is out of his scientific depth if he simply decides that Lucille had come to the conclusion that assisting at an abortion is morally wrong. That is surely not what the story was about. Actually, from the story we have no way of judging what decisions she will make about that. At best we can see some trajectory in her life story which says that she will presumably be more authentically herself in the future. But we don't know that she will or what shape her actions may take.

The psychological factor certainly has something to do with the story. The story tells of the roots of her decisions in childhood with a religious mother. Those reactions certainly did not come from her professional training. As a girl she experienced the shock of a God who seemed unconcerned about his faithful servant. That explains a good deal about Lucille though certainly it confuses the picture about God.

Probably the most unexplained psychological factor was Lucille's honesty. It did not take her long to admit that her tiff with Judy was mostly bluster. She was not really angry with Judy. Neither was her final experience something that she reasoned to. She never reasoned to the fact that she was an honest woman. That was simply there. She would not sacrifice her honesty no matter how uncomfortable it was. Her neighbors helped her, but that was only reinforcement of something which was already present.

So if we abandon the psychological approach and concentrate on this as a story, what do we have? Is it a hero story? In a way. Lucille is a hero and has achieved a victory. However, the cause and effect has not been explained to us in the story as should happen in a hero story. Is it a tragedy? It has some sad parts. We sympathize with her in her suffering. Tragedy should stir up pathos—and it does. And yet in the end it is not a tragedy, for tragedy destroys. Is it a comedy? Is it some quirk of God's breaking in on a person who is not even aware of who is knocking at the door? One must admit that Lucille ended with virtue and that is on the side of the angels.

The process of the tale centers on images—a manipulating friend, two doctors, one sympathetic and one not, a childhood picture of a deathbed scene vividly etched on the memory, a vision of peacefulness and order in a brick wall. The dynamic which moves the story along is always presented in images, and the images are always in conflict.

We set out to discover something about how the Bible influences us in our decision-making. Lucille never consciously adverts to the Bible. The closest she comes is to those popularized theologies of her mother, of a cliché from AA, and of the Clancys' faith. Perhaps we should pause here to ask if there is anything like this in the Bible. There are many parallels but one needs an artist's hand to pick out the illuminating ones. We need something which is full of human emotions of anger and guilt and accusation.

When Jacob after a checkered career as a con man and as a victim of a family feud came back toward his homeland, he reached the river Jabbok (Gen 32:23–33). He sent his numerous family and servants ahead of him across the river and remained alone in that gloomy canyon overnight. The story wants to say something of Jacob fighting his own demons of guilt, deception and thoughts of glory. So the author uses the myth of the river demon who will not let anyone pass in the night. Jacob and "an angel" fought with one another until dawn. Near dawn Jacob was about to overcome the angel, but the angel in one last effort wounded Jacob in the thigh. Then the dawn came and the angel (or demon) had to leave. But before he did, the "man" called him "Israel [you contended with God] because you have contended with divine and human beings and have prevailed" (Gen 32:29). But when Jacob wanted to know what was the man's name, he could not get it from him. Nevertheless, Jacob called the place Peniel ("face of God") "because I have seen God face to face and yet my life has been spared" (Gen 32:31).

The story is a marvel of popular insight into the relations of a chosen one and Yahweh. The mingling of the human and the divine is striking in this explanation of a change not just in name but in the character of Jacob. He is no longer the man he was. On his way to Mesopotamia many years before, Jacob had seen a ladder going up to heaven. At that time he was a huckster in religion. He said he would believe in God if his fortune turned out to be good (Gen 28:10–22). After the Jabbok incident Jacob was a believer. Jacob believed in a God he could not see, but whom he was sure that he had met. He had more to learn later, but he was on the way.

So also in the story of Lucille. She thought that she was looking at a brick wall. Jacob thought he was fighting a river demon. She was seeing God. That this God was shadowy and clothed in mysterious forms was as far as she got. But she was on the way to a new self.

God made himself present through his peace. That is one of the more usual signs of the presence of God. In the biblical tradition God is the God of peace. Jesus promises peace (Jn 14:27; 20:19) and Paul makes capital of it (1 Cor 7:15). In the history of Christian spirituality peace has always been the final sign of discerning God's will. Peace does not abolish the problems; it simply focuses our necessary faith on the right person. That is the conclusion of our rhetorical understanding; we are persuaded by our experience that we are good. It begins with faith; it ends with an assurance that we can make the right choices to be good.

Paul in Romans says of the consequences of faith: "Therefore, since we have been justified by faith, we have peace with God through our Lord Jesus Christ, through whom we have gained access [by faith] to this grace in which we stand, and we boast in hope of the glory of God. Not only that, but we even boast of our afflictions, knowing that affliction produces endurance, and endurance, proven character, and proven character, hope, and hope does not disappoint, because the love of God has been poured out in our hearts through the holy Spirit that has been given us" (Rom 5:1–5).

It is not the law which dictates what is right and wrong or which makes us righteous; it is our own consciousness that we are God's children which determines our goodness. It is not "self-image" in a psychological sense; it is the reality of our existence as known by faith. If one believes that the peace which comes from belief in God is simply another psychological reaction, perhaps a *stasis* condition from too much emotion, then that is an act of faith in psychological conclusions which we don't really know are true. If one believes, as Qoheleth did, that God gathers up the pieces so that nothing is lost (cf. Eccl 3:15), then that is an act of faith. The problem is to see either alternative as an act of faith and to choose which faith one really accepts.

In Christian ethics with its philosophical background of natural and supernatural existence, one says: grace. But is grace just a cellophane-wrapped entity all by itself? How is it packaged with all those human emotions? Lucille first had faith in her revolt against the religion of her mother. She thought that she gave up religion at the moment her mother died. The image of that one terrible deed remained with her. As the old doctor perceived, she did not understand a total judgment on the goodness of either her mother or of God. She was stuck on a single point of what she thought was right or wrong.

I have mentioned in prophetic preaching that no true prophet is simply a prophet of consolation or of doom. That is simplistic in our real life situations. True prophets who speak the word of God are both—at the same time. That is the conflict element which gives their sermons appeal. In our story it is the playing off of one emotion against another which allows the plot to develop. Without that factor Lucille forever remains in a hospital corridor thinking smoldering thoughts about her professional colleagues. With the faith element one gets into a different ambit of judgment. Lucille did not understand her experience as simply a matter of right and wrong. She went through her feelings of guilt, which some might label conscience, but it was much more a consciousness of who she was which was being weighed. She experienced it alone. The story has no other major character—a husband, a child, a professional colleague, a mentor. Her faith was not in some other human being; the Clancys helped, but that was all.

Such faith may very well co-exist with doubts about specific moral actions; only rarely do we have the unquestioned help of our neighbors in the church and its tradition to tell us absolutely what we should do. Yet we must judge, and we judge best on the basis of who we see that we are in the light of the unveiling of the mystery beyond us as we experience it. Such was Lucille's experience.

10

Conclusion

These simple reflections are not proposed as definitive of anything. If they help you examine your own experience and ask how you decided as a Christian, they have achieved their end.

Our daily decisions need to be reasonable. Ethicists operate on that level and are to be honored for the help which they give in understanding the facts and implications of problems. The church also is a teacher. Its teachings are not based on reason alone but also on faith, however tentative and much removed that may be from the basic beliefs. But the decision must be made by the individual.

In the long run, we are all doubtful about how good our decisions are. They are part of our story, and the story is not yet finished. So we do not know how well they fit into the total drama. Giving an alcoholic ten dollars for another bottle may seem both unreasonable and un-Christian. It only makes things worse. But perhaps things must get worse. Recovering alcoholics know that there is such a thing as hitting bottom. Before that time nothing seems to help. At the proper time something happens, but it is not caused by reasons. However, when that time is, no one knows except the alcoholic after it happens.

Most important to Christians is the awareness of mystery. We do not know precisely where it all ends. The Bible says that often enough. We have some inklings in the resurrection of Christ, but not enough to make all our judgments. Our best question is to keep asking ourselves: "Where is God in this mess?"

This book has tried to trace a path through the decisions which we Christians make on the basis of faith. The process begins usually with images of ourselves, what we think we are and what we would like to be—or not like to be. But these images are in conflict with one another somewhere, and that causes our problem. Locating the precise point of the conflict is most important. But the conflict does not stop. Indeed, it is escalated into a larger conflict, one that involves a struggle between good and evil and is larger than we are. Since the good is not immediately available to us (as in a reasonable decision), we need to make an act of faith that it actually exists. We cannot prove that any action will bring us to heaven or to hell—we do not know by experience how such decisions are made. So we believe, and in the believing we define one more trait in ourselves and surprisingly in the God whom we accept without knowing who he finally is.

The Christian decision is always a challenge. It challenges our pre-conceived ideas since it takes us so far beyond them. But it is a challenge to identity, to rising to the practical level of saying, "I am truly a son, a daughter of God." Paul knew that. After his very pragmatic and reasonable admonition at the end of 2 Corinthians he says: "Examine yourselves to see whether you are living in faith. Test yourselves. Do you not realize that Jesus Christ is in you?—unless, of course, you have failed the test" (2 Cor 13:5).

Notes

2. CONVINCED OR PERSUADED?

1. Robert Alter in the Introduction to *The Literary Guide to the Bible* (Robert Alter and Frank Kermode, Cambridge: Harvard University Press, 1987), 1–38 is the most recent study. Alter emphasizes how the biblical literature has infiltrated our whole cultural heritage. This has been a common observation for centuries.

2. *Britannica*, *Micropaedia*, "Rhetoric" has a sufficiently pointed and clear description for our purposes.

3. Bernard F. Lonergan, *Method in Theology* (New York: Herder & Herder, 1972), 6 is very interested in the "non-logical" aspects of method. He notes: "Our preliminary notion conceives method not as a set of rules but as a prior, normative pattern of operations from which the rules may be derived. Further, the operations envisaged are not limited to strictly logical operations, that is, to operations on propositions, terms, relations. It includes such operations, of course, for it speaks of describing, of formulating problems and hypotheses, of deducing implications. But it does not hesitate to move outside this group and to speak of inquiry, observation, discovery, experiment, synthesis, verification.

"Thirdly, what precisely these non-logical operations are, will concern us in the next section. But at once it may be noted that modern science derives its distinctive character from this grouping together of logical and non-logical operations. The logical tend to consolidate what has been achieved. The non-logical keep all achievement open to further advance. The conjunction of the two results in an open, ongoing, progressive and cumulative process. This process contrasts sharply not only with the static fixity that resulted from Aristotle's concentration on the necessary and immutable but also with Hegel's dialectic which is a movement enclosed within a complete system."

Later on Lonergan speaks of the difference between ordinary language and literary language, which also touches upon the difference between the various ways of logic or persuasion. These are essential elements of Lonergan's "transcendental method"; they will also be important in this book.

4. B. Jowett, *The Dialogues of Plato* (New York: Random House, 1982), Vol. 1, "Gorgias," 505–590. In the dialogue with Gorgias the rhetorician, Plato has Socrates take a very dim view of rhetoric. "In my opinion then, Gorgias, the whole of which rhetoric is a part is not an art at all, but the habit of a bold and ready wit, which knows how to manage mankind: this habit I sum up under the word 'flattery'; and it appears to me to have many other parts, one of which is cookery, which may seem to be an art, but, as I maintain, is only an experience and not an art—and the art of attiring and sophistry are two others" (521). In his next breath Socrates defines rhetoric as "the ghost or counterfeit of a part of politics" (522). It is noteworthy, however, that Plato himself used a dramatic, rhetorical style to present his ideas.

5. The assessment on the development of Christian ethics and Catholic moral theology is commonplace. Cf. such diverse authors as Charles E. Curran, *Moral Theology: A Continuing Journey* (Notre Dame: Notre Dame Press, 1982, Introduction), and R.E.O. White, *Christian Ethics, The Historical Development* (Atlanta: John Knox, 1981).

6. Williams C. Spohn, *What Are They Saying About Scripture and Ethics?* (New York: Paulist, 1984), 8.

7. Spohn, op. cit., 19–35, has an excellent chapter on Bonhoffer, Bultmann and Barth. Spohn's book is consistently good and shall be referred to frequently.

8. Vatican Council II, *Optatam Totius*, Decree on Priestly Formation, #16. "Special attention needs to be given to the development of moral theology. Its scientific exposition should be more thoroughly nourished by scriptural teaching. It should show the nobility of the Christian vocation of the faithful, and their obligation to bring forth fruit in charity for the life of the world." This is the only statement which the council made about ethics or moral theology, and it seems innocuous enough. However, it was the achievement of Josef Fuchs and under his leadership both in the council and in academic moral theology that this teaching has become a focal point for new developments in Catholic moral teaching.

9. Charles E. Curran and Richard A. McCormick, S.J, eds., *Readings in Moral Theology, No. 2, The Distinctiveness of Christian Ethics* (New York: Paulist, 1980), gather together sufficient of the current debate with chapters by such authors as Josef Fuchs, "Is There a Specifically Christian Morality?", Bruno Schiller, "The Debate on the Specific Character of a Christian Ethics: Some Remarks", James A. Gustafson, "Can Ethics be Christian?", etc. The debate may be interminable.

10. The involvement of scriptural analysis in the whole process of moral discernment was a major point in Robert Daly, *Christian Biblical Ethics* (New York: Paulist, 1984). Cf. pp. 117–131 for a full explanation.

11. Cf. Robert Alter and Frank Kermode, *The Literary Guide to the Bible* (Cambridge: Harvard University Press, 1987), for a recent and popular study.

12. Terence Keegan, O.P., *Interpreting the Bible* (New York: Paulist, 1985), 81, has an interesting personal note: "At the

1981 annual meeting of the Catholic Biblical Association there was a panel headed by Raymond Brown that made an impassioned plea for the retention of the historical-critical method as the mainstay of Catholic biblical studies. A fundamental concern expressed by members of that panel was that other methods being introduced were less certain, less objective than was the historical critical method."

13. Gabriel Fackre, "Positive Values and Honorable Intentions, A Critique of Fundamentalism," *New Theology Review*, 1 (1988), 58–71, has an excellent and sympathetic analysis of contemporary fundamentalism.

14. Peter D. Miscall, *1 Samuel: A Literary Reading* (Bloomington: Indiana State University Press, 1986), 166–72. Miscall does not arrive at the same conclusion as I have used here, but his method is somewhat similar.

15. Cf. James A. Fischer, "Ethics and Wisdom," *Catholic Biblical Quarterly*, 40 (1978), 303.

3. IMAGES

1. Oscar Wilde, *The Picture of Dorian Gray* (1890). When Wilde's only novel first appeared in *Lippincott's Monthly Magazine*, it was furiously denounced as degrading, immoral and valueless. When the dust settled the next year, Walter Pater found the book to have a very clear moral, a denunciation of epicurianism in British society. Much later (1918) H.L. Menken analyzed Wilde as a bogus Puritan with an uncanny ability to do rare and lovely things with words. Wilde himself seems to have sensed something of this. Near the beginning of Dorian Gray he has the painter Hallward demand that his portrait never be displayed for it reveals too much of himself. Perhaps Wilde was trying to hide behind his character. Cf. Karl Beckson, ed., *Oscar Wilde, The Critical Heritage* (New York: Barnes & Noble, 1970).

2. Emil G. Kraeling, *I Have Kept the Faith: The Life of the Apostle Paul* (Chicago: Rand & McNally, 1965).

3. William C. Spohn, *What Are They Saying about Scripture and Ethics?* (New York: Paulist, 1983), 46–50, summarizes the positions of Rahner and Fuchs excellently.

4. Cf. H. Edward Everding, Jr. and Dana Wilbanks, *Decision Making in the Bible* (Valley Forge: Judson, 1975), especially Chapter 6, "Communal Context," 105–130, for a good example.

5. For a classic analysis of how we do use scripture, cf. James Gustafson, "The Place of Scripture in Christian Ethics: A Methodological Study," *Interpretation* 24 (1970), 430–55, in which this exemplar approach is the first method described. The corrective is Gustafson's fourth method which insists on using the Bible as a whole.

6. For a popular contemporary statement cf. Joseph Campbell with Bill Moyers, *The Power of Myth* (New York: Doubleday, 1988). This is a derivative from a popular Public Broadcasting System TV series. Joseph Campbell's originating work was entitled *The Hero with a Thousand Faces* (Princeton: Princeton University Press, 1949).

7. Joseph Campbell, *Hero*, Preface and 387–91, and *The Power of Myth* (New York: Doubleday, 1988), 3–35. One does not need to become an expert in mythology to appreciate what is being said here. *Britannica, Macropaedia* has a sufficient article on myth to illustrate the power of myth to leap the centuries. Nor need one espouse a particular psychological explanation, such as that of Freud or Jung, to appreciate the significance of transhistorical insight. The myths are so widespread and so concentrated on certain subjects and ways of expressing them that one must conclude that there is some commonality among us all which makes them endlessly appealing. The point here is not the dependence of biblical stories on myth—that would be historical criticism in its source-critical phase—but simply the

ability of myth along with other literature to form a connective between then and now.

8. Bernard Lonergan's "Method in Theology" involves an hermeneutical circle from Phase I which begins with experience through understanding into judgment and decision and finally to conversion. For a descriptive figure, cf. Patrick Corcoran, *Looking at Lonergan's Method* (Dublin: Talbot, 1975).

9. Robert Daly, *Christian Biblical Ethics*, 114–138, gives a great deal of attention to the "hermeneutical circle."

10. The classic work is Sir James George Frazer, *The Golden Bough* (New York: St. Martin's, 1966; original edition, 1890), 13 vols. Cf. also Theodor H. Gaster, *The New Golden Bough* (New York: Criterion, 1959), and, more specifically, *Myth, Legend and Custom in the Old Testament* (New York: Harper and Row, 1969), especially the Introduction, xxv–lv.

11. Cf. Terence J. Keegan, O.P., *Interpreting the Bible* (New York: Paulist, 1985), Chapter 4, "Structuralism," 40–72 for an excellent brief survey of structuralism.

12. Vatican II, *Gaudium et Spes*, #12. Cf. Austin Flannery, *Vatican Council II* (Wilmington: Scholarly Resources, 1975), 363.

13. Josef Fuchs, "Christian Morality: Biblical Orientation and Human Evaluation," *Gregorianum* 67 (1986), 745–63.

14. Theodor Gaster, *The Oldest Stories in the World* (New York: Viking, 1952) has a selection of pertinent mythological and hero stories. Gaster follows Stith Thompson's *Motif-Index of Folk Literature*, and relies also on FitzRoy Richard Summerset, Lord Raglan, *The Hero* (London: Methuen & Co., Ltd., 1936). Raglan, however, is not immediately concerned with mythological, but legendary stories. Gaster is similar to Joseph Campbell in his approach to mythology, but Gaster is a specialist in the mythological aspects of the Bible. His comments on the story of Master Good and Master Bad from a

Hittite source are particularly suggestive (cf. pp. 1267–71). Gaster comments that this theme of the exposed child is familiar from the legends of Moses, Sargon of Agade, Perseus, Oedipus, Paris, and Romulus and Remus. "Lord Raglan has pointed out that the tale of the child exposed or spirited away and subsequently rescued by chance is a standard element in the sagas of great gods or national heroes in all civilizations, recurring—to cite but a few instances—in the myths of Zeus, Asclepius, Apollo, Dionysius, and Jason among the Greeks, and in those of Arthur and Llew Llawgyffes among the British and Welsh respectively" (170). One may suspect that this pattern is behind the way in which Matthew arrayed his material for the infancy account.

4. CONFLICT

1. Cf. Paul D. Duke, *Irony in the Fourth Gospel* (Atlanta: John Knox, 1985), 7–28, for a good general treatment, and Alan Culpepper, *Anatomy of the Fourth Gospel* (Philadelphia: Fortress, 1983), especially Chapter 1 for a general overview justifying rhetorical criticism in this matter, or pp. 161–62 for examples of misunderstandings.

2. Cf. James A. Fischer, "Pauline Literary Forms and Thought Patterns," *Catholic Biblical Quarterly* 39 (1977), 209–23.

3. Josef Fuchs, *Christian Morality: The Word Becomes Flesh* (Dublin: Gill & Macmillan, Georgetown University Press, 1987), 83–101.

4. Robert Gordis, *Mequillat Esther* (New York: KTAV, 1974), has a very intelligent defense of Esther as a canonical book from the viewpoint of illustrating God's preservative will for his chosen people.

5. The interpretation of Romans 7:7–8:1 as personal experi-

ence is certainly not the common one. Commentators are more inclined to interpret the experience as a generic one of the whole human race or of Paul before his conversion. J.A.T. Robinson, *Wrestling with Romans* (Philadelphia: Westminster, 1979), 82–91, gives a lengthy review of the opinions. Then he comes down on the side of present experience which is both personal and typical. I think that the same is verified by a rhetorical analysis of the passage.

6. Bernard Häring, *The Law of Christ*, 3 vols. (Westminster: Newman, 1961–66), was the first Catholic attempt in recent time to organize Christian morality around the love commandment. Cf. Jack T. Sanders, *Ethics in the New Testament* (Philadelphia: Fortress, 1975), Chapter 1 and the Epilogue for a rather scathing critique of the love theme. "Will ethicists continue to publish still more works predicated on the false assumption that the command to love is some kind of norm or middle axiom laid down as a law that is valid for all times? (a notion which this study should lay to rest, although I have no false hopes). Can theologians and philosophers reflect (a few are still able) on the validity of the concept of qualitatively transcendent love and the implications of such a notion? These would appear to be the alternatives remaining. Otherwise, throw out the New Testament as an aid to ethics once and for all" (129). Jacques Ellul, *The Ethics of Freedom* (Grand Rapids: Eerdmans, 1976), Gerhard von Rad, *Old Testament Theology* (New York: Harper and Row, 1962) on covenant, and Samuel Terrien, *The Elusive Presence* (San Francisco: Harper and Row, 1978) have made notable efforts to organize biblical theology around some central theme, such as liberty or response to God or presence.

7. Joseph Campbell, *The Hero with a Thousand Faces* (Princeton: Princeton University Press, first edition 1949; third printing 1973).

5. FAITH

1. A discussion of *sensus plenior* as of 1968 can be found in the Raymond Brown, Joseph Fitzmyer, Roland Murphy, eds., *Jerome Biblical Commentary* (Englewood Cliffs: Prentice-Hall, 1968), 71:56–70 by Raymond Brown.

2. Cf. Raymond Collins, *Introduction to the New Testament* (Garden City: Doubleday, 1983), 317–55 for a recent full statement on a Catholic understanding of inspiration. Thomas Hoffman, "Inspiration, Normativeness, Canonicity and the Unique Sacred Character of the Bible," in *Catholic Biblical Quarterly*, 44 (1982), 447–69 offers an excellent statement from a Thomistic viewpoint.

3. Raymond E. Brown, *The Birth of the Messiah* (Garden City: Doubleday, 1977), 143–155 has an exhaustive treatment of these verses both in Isaiah and in Matthew. The textual problem of "the virgin" has been known from antiquity and is not really crucial for our consideration. The understanding of "fulfilled" is much more the modern problem.

4. My citations are from the New American Bible. Other recent translations are not radically different; sometimes "young woman" is used for *parthenos*, which in Greek is the proper word for "virgin." Brown, op. cit. in a footnote on p. 146 (no. 37), recalls that the Catholic translators of NAB, of whom he was one, wanted to translate the word as "young woman" but were restrained by a decision of the American bishops.

5. Council of Ephesus, 431 A.D., Roy J. Deferrari, ed., *Denziger, The Sources of Catholic Dogma* (St. Louis: Herder, 1957), 50. "If anyone does not confess that God is truly Emmanuel, and that on this account the Holy Virgin is the Mother of God (for according to the flesh she gave birth to the Word of God become flesh by birth), let him be anathema" (Decree 113). The text of the Council clearly depends on Mat-

thew and Luke with an additional nod toward John. "Mother of God," however, is a daring step forward.

6. Madeleine Boucher, *The Mysterious Parable* [Catholic Biblical Quarterly Monograph Series 6 (1977)].

7. William C. Spohn, S.J., *What Are They Saying About Scripture and Ethics?* (New York: Paulist, 1984), 89–105 has a chapter on this approach as exemplified by Hauerwas, McFague and Yoder—which may not be the best selection, but illustrates the approach.

8. Joseph Campbell, *The Power of Myth* (New York: Doubleday, 1988).

9. The problem of the ending of Mark is well known. Mark 16:1–8 is the original. Mark 16:9–20, the summary stories of the appearance to Mary Magdalene, the disciples on the road to Emmaus, and the first appearance of Jesus to the eleven plus the commission to preach the good news and baptize and the ascension, is admittedly a later addition. However, it is traditionally part of the canonical text. One cannot interpret the final meaning of Mark's gospel as confusion about his first verse: "Here begins the gospel of Jesus Christ, the Son of God" (Mk 1:1). The gospel as a whole has no bewilderment or trembling about who Jesus was. The canonical tradition must govern the interpretation of the final original verses. On the other hand, the Shorter Ending (Mk 16, one verse after v. 20) and the Freer Logion (Mk 16, three or four verses) are not found in the best manuscripts and do not form part of the canonical text. They represent a later and much less certain tradition.

10. Cf. Terence Keegan, *Interpreting the Bible* (New York: Paulist, 1985), 83–85 for a good, but concise explanation of reader-response criticism.

11. Paul Watzlawick, John H. Weakland, Richard Fisch, *Change: Principles of Problem Formation and Problem Resolution* (New York: W.W. Norton, 1974), 72.

12. Paul Watzlawick, Janet H. Beavin, Don D. Jackson, *Pragmatics of Human Communication: A Study of International Patterns, Pathologies, and Paradoxes* (New York: W.W. Norton, 1967), 253.

13. Watzlawick, *Pragmatics,* 254.

14. Carol Gilligan, *In a Different Voice* (Cambridge: Harvard University Press, 1982), and Nell Noddings, *Caring—A Feminine Approach to Ethics and Moral Education* (Berkeley: University of California, 1984).

15. Cf. Philip Keane, *Christian Ethics and Imagination* (New York: Paulist, 1984) as an attempt to use pastoral experience in the imaging of moral problems and coordinate with scientific ethics and morality. This brings in some of the feminine insights.

16. Matthew 5:48 in the NAB translation reads: "In a word, you must be made perfect as your heavenly Father is perfect." This does less than justice to the text and context. Our older English translation read: "Be perfect as your heavenly Father is perfect." That read well with Matthew 5:17: "I have come to fulfill (perfect) the law." Although *plerosai* is used in verse 17 and *teleioi* in verse 48, both words have the meaning of bringing to completion. Moreover, the pattern of the arrangement of the chapter is familiar: first comes an announcement of the subject (Mt 5:17), then a series of antitheses (Mt 5:21–47), and then the summary punch line. Paul uses a similar technique in 1 Corinthians 7:29–31. The NAB Revised New Testament returns to the earlier reading.

17. Markus Barth, *Ephesians 4–6* (AB, Garden City: Doubleday, 1974), 758ff, has a lengthy treatise on the *Haustafeln* which espouses this view. He notes that there are also Mesopotamian sources for the *Haustafeln*, but that the dependence is more probably on rabbinic sources.

18. The Greek word "submissive" has provoked much misunderstanding and emotion in our day. Basically, the word

refers to order. Its root is *tage* which is a military expression for a formation of soldiers. The derivatives are images of proper stances and relationships. So Christ is said to be submissive to the Father (1 Cor 15:28); we are to be submissive to one another (Eph 5:21) and to the leaders of the community (1 Cor 16:16). In the *Haustafeln* the reference is undoubtedly to the accepted deference of wives to the decisions of their husbands. However, the point being made is that one can see a potential for imitating Christ in these domestic customs.

19. Markus Barth, *Ephesians 4–6*, 758.

20. Cf. James A. Fischer, "Politics and Biblical Ethics: Romans 13:1–7," in *Christian Biblical Ethics* for an illustration.

21. Cf. William C. Spohn, S.J., *What Are They Saying About Scripture and Ethics?* (New York: Paulist, 1984), Chapter Two, "Scripture as Moral Reminder," which describes the approach of Josef Fuchs, Karl Rahner and Bruno Schuller as particularly helpful.

22. Cf. Joseph Campbell, *The Power of Myth*, on mythological hero stories.

6. THE PERSON

1. Arthur C. Clarke, *2001, A Space Odyssey* (New York: Signet, 1968). The novel, which was adapted from the movie, brings out much more clearly the myth of Odysseus, the wayfarer from the Trojan War, in his attempts to reach home. The theme is a common one in mythology; it pictures mankind's attempt to reach the God from whom we came.

2. Samuel Terrien, *The Elusive Presence* (New York: Harper & Row, 1978).

3. Cf. for example, covenant/promise by Gerhard Von Rad, salvation history by Otto Procksch and prevalent in the writings of Vatican Council II, "God Who Acts" by George E.

Wright, love by Bernard Häring, freedom by Jacques Ellul, etc.

4. Cf. Kristar Stendahl, "Biblical Theology," in George A. Buttrick (ed.), *Interpreter's Dictionary of the Bible*, 418–432. This is considered the classical statement.

5. Joseph Campbell, *The Power of Myth* (New York: Doubleday, 1988), 207ff, denies this for non-western myth. Moyers had asked the question: "And your life comes from where?" Campbell responded: "From the ultimate energy that is the life of the universe. And then do you say, 'Well, there must be somebody generating that energy'? Why do you have to say that? Why can't the ultimate mystery be impersonal?" Moyers pressed on: "Can men and women live with an impersonality?" and Campbell answered: "Yes, they do all over the place. Just go east of Suez. You know there is this tendency in the West to anthropomorphize and accent the humanity of the gods, the personifications. . . ." The factual data is there, although the reference to Suez lands us right in the middle of the area that saw the origin of the three great religions of Judaism, Christianity and Mohammedanism; they all have personal gods. More to the point, however, is the importance of the personal gods. In our tradition without a person, there is no law-giver and there is no possibility of an effective ethic. There is no one to discover behind the law. As we shall see in Chapter Eight, there is also no end or meaning to life. The world and our personal selves are eventually all swallowed up in either nothingness or everything. Personal existence as a present experience is a meaningless concept.

6. Cf. *Theological Dictionary of the New Testament*, II, 541–43 which notes that Paul's use of the phrase is unique and cannot be traced to either pagan or Jewish sources. For a more recent investigation cf. A.J.M. Wedderburn, "Some Observations on Paul's Use of the Phrases 'in Christ' and 'with Christ,' " *Journal for the Study of the New Testament*, 25 (1985), 83–97.

Wedderburn notes that Schnelle (1983) has recently proposed that Paul used the expression on the analogy of Christ as the figure of wisdom, and admits that he may well be correct (88).

7. Cf. Rom 8:29; 2 Cor 3:18; 4:4; Col 1:15; 3:10, the last of which is a good example: "Put on the new self, which is being renewed, for knowledge, in the image of its creator."

8. Paul Minear, *Images of the Church in the New Testament* (Philadelphia: Westminster, 1960). Minear studied over a hundred images which are used to describe the church.

9. Karl Rahner, *Inspiration in the Bible* (New York: Herder & Herder, 1964). Rahner's treatment of the Bible as the foundational document of the church led Catholics to new views of inspiration and canonicity.

10. Cf. Terence J. Keegan, *Interpreting the Bible* (New York: Paulist, 1985), 131–44 for a fine analysis of canonical criticism. Brevard Childs has been the principal scholar in the study; cf. Brevard Childs, *Introduction to the Old Testament as Scripture* (Philadelphia: Fortress, 1979); *The New Testament as Canon: An Introduction* (Philadelphia: Fortress, 1977).

11. Albert Sundberg, Jr. "The Bible Canon and the Christian Doctrine of Inspiration," *Interpretation* 29 (1975), 352–71. Sundberg has been the most persistent and perspicacious student of canon from an historical viewpoint.

12. Vatican Council II, *Dei Verbum*, Revelation, n. 11. Cf. Austin Flannery, *Vatican Council II*, 756–57, on inspiration and inerrancy.

13. Josef Fuchs, *Christian Morality: The Word Becomes Flesh* (Dublin: Gill and Macmillan, Georgetown University Press, 1987), 14–17.

14. Vatican Council II, *Lumen Gentium*, The Church, n. 12. Cf. Austin Flannery, *Vatican Council II*, 363: "The whole body of the faithful who have an anointing that comes from the holy one cannot err in matters of belief."

15. The meaning of the text has been consistently questioned

throughout history. TDNT, I, 716 defines *suggnome* as "agreement, forbearance, pardon." Then it remarks about 1 Corinthians 7:6: "Though the context might support 'personal opinion', there is no example of this. *gnome* is the word used in such cases." Cf. 1 Cor 7:40 for this use of *gnome*. However, the remark about context is useful whatever the meaning of *suggnome*. Robertson and Plummer in the ICC commentary on 1 Corinthians remark that "the word occurs nowhere else in the New Testament and is very rare." Moulton-Milligan and Liddell-Scott confirm this. Moulton-Milligan observe that from the meaning "allowance for circumstances" there is an easy transition to the sense of pardon in the papyri. However, the examples given all are of the literary genus: "pardon me for this . . ." As TDNT remarks, the context supports "personal opinion" and the indulgence Paul asks is for his opinion, not for the sexual partners. Either that or he is just giving advice. *Thesarus Linguae Latinae* on *indulgentia* notes that the basic meaning of the Latin word is that of giving help, favor, etc. However, by the time of the Council of Chalcedon (451 A.D.) the word was being used of the action of a bishop in giving "permission" for a monk to leave a monastery. Jerome, *Contra Jovinum*, 1, 8 comments on our verse: "Nuptias non vocare indulgentiam, sed imperium," in the sense that among the gifts given to the faithful marriage is not a permission, but a command. The Latin mind seems to have become fixed after the fourth century.

    16. Robert Daly, *Christian Biblical Ethics* (New York: Paulist, 1984), 14.

    17. Daly, *Ethics*, 294.

    18. H. Edward Everding and Dana Willbanks, *Decision Making and the Bible* (Valley Forge: Judson, 1975). Also Paul Achtemeier, *The Inspiration of Scripture: Problems and Proposals* (Philadelphia: Westminster, 1980).

    19. E. Gerstenberger, "Covenant and Commandment," *JBL* 84 (1965), 38–58.

20. Robert Daly, *Christian Biblical Ethics*, 45–54.

21. An example of this kind of personal decision-making is given in *Christian Biblical Ethics*, pp. 256–65, "Dissent Within a Religious Community: Romans 9–11" by James A. Fischer. The occasion was a personal problem of the author. One can expect neither agreement nor certitude in such matters. All one can do is to put one's personal honesty on the line. The method used is basically parallel to that of Bernard Lonergan in *Method in Theology;* cf. Bernard F. Lonergan, *Method in Theology* (New York: Herder & Herder, 1972).

7. HOW DO THEY SAY IT?

1. Cf. *Christian Biblical Ethics*, James A. Fischer, Chapter 4, "Story and Image," 156–69 for a fuller discussion.

2. Cf. Luis Alonso Schokel, *The Inspired Word* (New York: Herder, 1965), 151–73 for an excellent treatment of these levels of language.

3. Terence J. Keegan, O.P., *Interpreting the Bible* (New York: Paulist, 1985), 92–109, has a brief but precise description of narrative theology in biblical studies.

4. James A. Fischer, *How To Read the Bible* (New York: Dodd & Mead, 1987, rev. ed.), 47–64, describes these types in more detail.

5. Bernard Lonergan, *Method in Theology* (New York: Herder and Herder, 1972), 72.

6. Cf. Norman Gottwald, *Studies in the Book of Lamentations* (London: SCM, 1954), 109. Indeed this theme is seen as central throughout the study.

7. Cf. Robert Alter and Frank Kermode, *The Literary Guide to the Bible* (Cambridge: MA: Harvard University Press, 1987). The authors in their introduction term this study "literary criticism," and that is surely an accurate description. However, the term has already been appropriated in historical criti-

cism of the Bible with a quite different meaning. I have preferred the more distinctive and traditional phrase "rhetorical criticism." However, we are talking of the same thing. Alter also gives a good brief introduction to the emerging history of this literary criticism, dating it from Erich Auerbach's *Mimnesis*, published in 1918. Cf. Terrence Keegan, *Interpreting the Bible* (New York: Paulist, 1985), for an excellent description of the various kinds of rhetorical criticism which are currently in use. The perioidical *Semeia* is devoted to this study.

8. *Optatum Totius*, "The Training of Priests," n. 16. Cf. Austin Flannery, O.P. *Vatican Council II* (Wilmington: Scholarly Resources, 1975), 720.

8. ESCHATOLOGY AND APOCALYPTIC

1. William Spohn, *What Are They Saying About Scripture and Ethics?* (New York: Paulist, 1984), 46–48, has a brief description of Rahner's position.

2. The thesis that the earliest Christians expected an imminent *parousia* seems to be the "standard" view. For example, Norman Perrin, *The New Testament: An Introduction* (New York: Harcourt, Brace & Jovanovich, 1974), has much to say about apocalyptic; in fact, he almost interprets the New Testament—certainly Mark—from this viewpoint (cf. Ch. 4, "Apocalyptic Christianity," 65–87; Ch. 7, "The Gospel of Mark," 143–167—which follows Marxsen in its interpretation). He takes for granted that early Christianity accepted an imminent parousia (pp. 74–77 for Q as basically eschatological and p. 144 for Mark). He presumes that the early gospel preaching was apocalyptic in some way, but he has no clear evidence. He traces apocalyptic through Paul and into the primitive form of Mark 13 (although he does not go as far as Marxsen who divides Mark 13 into a pre-Markan apocalyptic pamphlet and a redactional Christian introduction to Mark's

church—which is not really a revolutionary idea; cf. Mally, *Jerome Biblical Commentary*, 42:76 from the 1960s)—and presumes that it blossomed again about 70 A.D. due to the destruction of Jerusalem.

John McKenzie in his *Dictionary of the Bible*, "Parousia," similarly has no doubt about imminent parousia: he asserts: "that the impression was common in the early Church seems to admit no doubt." None of the quotes he cites actually say anything decisive about "imminent," and McKenzie has not one reference to why he thinks this was a common opinion in the early church. So also Mally in *JBC* 42: 76.

Rudolf Schnackenburg, *The Moral Teaching of the New Testament* (New York: Seabury, 1979), 185–96, summarizes the New Testament by books on imminent parousia and concludes that "Catholic scholars admit that in the earliest epistles to the Churches, Paul seems to count seriously on the imminent coming of the Lord, believing that he himself and some of those he is addressing will see within their own lifetimes this act of God that will save the from all their tribulations" (p. 189) and "the idea of the parousia was by no means restricted to St. Paul alone; it was common property among the first Christians" (p. 192). Schnackenburg does not detail any evidence he has that it was common property among the first Christians.

3. D.S. Russell, *The Method and Message of Jewish Apocalyptic* (Philadelphia: Westminster, 1964), in his catalog of apocalyptic books of the first century A.D. lists only *The Life of Adam and Eve* and *The Apocalypse of Abraham* as possibly dating from around 70 A.D. The Slavonic *Book of Enoch* is too uncertain to pin down to this time. The other six books listed as dating from the first century A.D. don't qualify at all. So there seems no decisive evidence for a blossoming of apocalyptic about 70 A.D.

4. J.A.T. Robinson, *Redating the New Testament* (Philadel-

phia: Westminster, 1976), 13–30. This is an update of Robinson's views in *Jesus and His Coming*, (London: SCM, 1957). A.L. Moore, *The Parousia in the New Testament*, (Leiden: Brill, 1966), has an excellent survey in the *Supplements to Novum Testamentum*. Moore sees *parousia* more as a christological problem than a temporal one. More recently, Walter Kasper, "Coming of Jesus Christ," in *Communio* 12 (1985) 368–84 cites Karl Barth: "Thus the *Parousia* is not a temporal event, not a fantastic ending of the world; it has no connection with any eventual, historic, earthly, or cosmic catastrophe." So Kasper concludes that it is the christological concentration which is important in the New Testament, not the temporality. So also Richard N. Longnecker, "Paul's Early Eschatology," in *New Testament Studies* 31 (1985), 85–95, although he prefers to call it christological function. The academic emphasis seems to be swinging away from the "standard" view outlined above in note 1.

5. Opke in *Theological Dictionary of the New Testament* under "parousia" remarks that apocalyptic is saturated with a close expectation of the end, but it is not really a temporal prophecy. D.S. Russell exemplifies Jewish apocalypses with his comment on Daniel: "It is obvious that this book was written during and for the time of the End. 'The hour is at hand.' This is its abiding message—not its calculations and predictions and prognostications. All these are secondary to the conviction that the time is short and the End will speedily come" (*Method*, 264).

6. Russell, *Method*, 264 notes: "Even with the passing of the years and the non-appearance of the End, their faith did not falter." Opke remarks of Paul's use of imminent parousia: "The external fulfillment is not awaited for its own sake, but as an accompanying circumstance leading to full fellowship with God," and again, "It is not an historical event."

7. Kenneth R. Himes, "Scripture and Ethics: A Review Essay," *Biblical Theology Bulletin* 15 (1985), 65–73, gives a re-

cent review of theologians and biblicists' views on eschatology and ethics. It has been a common problem for many years.

8. For this summary evaluation, cf. Russell, *Method*, p. 269.

9. Rudolf Schnackenburg, *The Moral Teaching of the New Testament* (New York: Seabury, 1979), 378.

10. Cf. Robert Daly, *Christian Biblical Ethics*, 114–31.

11. E.g. Nell Noddings, *Caring: A Feminine Approach to Ethics and Moral Education* (Berkley: University of California Press, 1984). The problem arises if the supreme criterion of goodness is placed on the degree of caring for the other.

12. Ibid. 90–94.